JAPANESE MILITARY SAKE CUPS • 1894-1945

JAPANESE MILITARY SAKE CUPS

1894-1945

Dan King

Schiffer Military History
Atglen, PA

Special Thanks

I would like the following for their assistance without whose support this book would not have been possible: Steve Ackley, Sgt.Major Jim Dever, John Hastings, Bob Herron, Louis Foxwell, Richard Fuller, Chris Harrison, Shigeru Kajita, Don Kochi, Joseph Marino, John Mitchell, Gary Nila, Lynn McCready, Deidra Miltimore of Gekkeikan *Sake* USA, Mitsuyuki Oishi, James Oxnard, Bernie Pfister (WWII), Bob Rolfe, Kimihiko Sato, SSgt. Quay Terry, Ivan Prall (WWII), Akira Takizawa, Chuck Waud, Doss White, GnySgt Tom Williams, Jiro Yoshida (WWII), Nobuo Yoshioka. Finally, it was my father Marvin King, a former Korean War POW, and his long time collection of mug cups that sowed the seeds for this book.

Dedication

This book is dedicated to my two treasures,
Cindy and Jimmy.

Book design by Ian Robertson.

Library of Congress Catalog Number: 2003110834.

Printed in China.
ISBN: 0-7643-1881-0

Published by Schiffer Publishing Ltd.
4880 Lower Valley Road
Atglen, PA 19310
Phone: (610) 593-1777
FAX: (610) 593-2002
E-mail: Info@schifferbooks.com.
Visit our web site at: www.schifferbooks.com
Please write for a free catalog.
This book may be purchased from the publisher.
Please include $3.95 postage.
Try your bookstore first.

In Europe, Schiffer books are distributed by:
Bushwood Books
6 Marksbury Ave.
Kew Gardens
Surrey TW9 4JF
England
Phone: 44 (0)20 8392-8585
FAX: 44 (0)20 8392-9876
E-mail: Info@bushwoodbooks.co.uk.
Free postage in the UK. Europe: air mail at cost.
Try your bookstore first.

CONTENTS

INTRODUCTION

Due to a marked in interest in the Pacific Theater of Operations in World War II, and the popularity of on-line auctions we have witnessed a growing number of collectors, historians and World War II enthusiasts adding Japanese Military *sake* cups to their collections. The purpose of this work is to provide the reader with accurate information to aid in translating, determining the origin, value and history of the Japanese Military *Sake* Cups in his/her collection. It is hoped the book will foster a greater understanding and appreciation for this little known field of collecting.

• • •

I first became interested in the Japanese perspective on World War II during a summer spent in Fujisawa, Kamakura as an exchange student. I met a man who had been in the Imperial Japanese Cavalry in China during the late 1930s. I recall his faded horseback photos and *sake* cups with horse designs on his shelf. It was that meeting that sparked my interest in World War II Japan.

After high school I earned my degree in Japanese language from CSULA. One of my professors was Dr. Kato, who, at sixteen years old, had been an Army kamikaze pilot whose aircraft was destroyed in a B-29 bombing raid at the war's end. He recalled bitter tears of shame at being denied his final mission. It wasn't until after the war did he realize he had been brainwashed into almost throwing away his life against people he would come to deeply respect and later live among and educate.

After graduation, I went to work at a Japanese company for fifteen years, ten of them being in the city of Nagoya. Working in Japan helped me better grasp the language and to more fully understand the widely held opinions on the war.

I was fortunate enough to meet dozens of Japanese World War II veterans, who provided invaluable insight on the training, education, and life of Japanese soldiers and sailors. It was at this time I began collecting Japanese military *sake* cups. Although being a collector at heart, it was the *sake* cups more than the medals, uniforms and equipment that kept drawing me in with their delicate beauty and stories waiting to be told. It was my frustrated search for information on *sake* cups that began a journey of discovery of firsthand research. The result of which is this book.

Shiro Shimada and the author with an Imperial cup presented to Mr. Shimada, one of five survivors of the 800 man 9th regiment that was destroyed in the July 7 Banzai charge on Saipan.

1

MILITARY *SAKE* CUPS

Why the recent interest in Japanese military *sake* cups? One can think of five reasons for the increased interest in these historical items:

- They are genuine historical antiques from the 1890s-1940s with no fakes being produced. The cost would be prohibitive due to the time and skill necessary to make them. Who could imagine a seventy-five year old piece of militaria that needs no certificate of authenticity!
- They are of highest quality
- Each one is unique and involves old-world craftmanship in which no two are alike
- There is little information on them allowing for the collector to conduct firsthand research
- They are laughingly underpriced in comparison to their historic value and artwork making them a wise investment.

Collectors seek *sake* cups for different reasons; the intricate artwork, as fine examples of Japanese pottery, others see them as affordable World War II antiques to augment their collections, others see them as an investment, while others seek out cups from a specific subject such as machine guns or artillery or a specific regiment that appeals to them. Some collectors look for naval cups, or aviation cups, or cups that have name and rank listed. While others collect the popular "helmet

Soldiers of the 16 Division parade in a triumphant return to Nara station after a two-year tour in Manchuria, July 1936. (*Mainichi Shinbun*)

Soldiers presenting their commander with a final salute at a discharge ceremony, December 1936. (*Mainichi Shinbun*)

Friends and family members send off soldiers of the 3rd Regiment, December 1938. (*Mainichi Shinbun*)

cups" or the traditional red lacquer cups. Almost no two cups are alike so there is no risk of ever finding all of the variations and becoming bored. There is no 'collect all 10' with Japanese military *sake* cups. This hobby is a Zen-like journey with no definite end point as one can never own all of the variations of *sake* cups produced during Japan's period of attempted overseas expansion from 1894-1945.

As well known military researcher Richard Fuller writes, "Truly this is a field of collecting that sails into uncharted waters. Genuine bargains are really out there…and whatever you find it will be guaranteed to provide pleasure, research potential, be family friendly and won't break the bank in order to acquire." I could not have put it better!

The next question might be, "Why did the Japanese produce these military *sake* cups?"

The Japanese military machine had a plan to systematically conjure up images of the Nation's glorious samurai past through images familiar to the population. Examples include the use of samurai swords, samurai style long helmet straps, Imperial mum logos on weapons and the ceremonial consumption of *sake*.

Sake cups were commissioned to commemorate any number of events including, but not limited to, enlistment, promotions of rank, qualification badges, overseas naval cruise, overseas dispatch, home leave, victory parades, ship commissioning, valor awards, yearly war games, military term fulfillment, honorable discharge, short term recall, and even death in battle.

Many military *sake* cups list the owner's unit making identification possible. It is always interesting to find a *sake* cup from a regiment that was involved in a famous, or infamous, battle.

Japanese soldiers and sailors gave commemorative *sake* cups to friends, neighbors, comrades, and co-workers.[1] The commonly held belief in the West is that *sake* cups were distributed from the military only. While the military did present cups to the fighting man, most cups were commissioned by the soldiers and sailors to commemorate their own achievements or goals. The custom of presenting Military *sake* cups reached its peak during late 1930s when Japan was at her zenith of power. At that time her borders stretched across Korea, China, Manchuria, and parts of Russia. The earliest known examples of military *sake* cups the author has identified are from the 1894 Sino-Japan war. In addition to the 1894 Sino-Japan war, the author has located examples from the 1904-1905 Russo-Japan war; 1918-1922 Expedition to Russia; 1937-1945 China War; and the 1941-1945 Pacific War (the latter being some of the rarest).

Most *sake* cups are classified as the standard size *Guinomi* (drink quick) style, with the smaller cups being known as *Choko*. The word "*choko*" appears to be derived from the Korean word "*chonku*", which means "a small, shallow cup or dish".

Sake cups come in all sizes ranging from the tiny 1.5" across to the largest sizes that can reach 5" in diameter. Generally speaking, the larger the cup the rarer it is.

Notes:
[1] Personal interview during Veteran Reunion, author 1994

Japanese sailors and Petty Officers at an *izakeya* enjoying both beer and sake, Autumn 1943. (*Chuck Waud*)

2

SAKE AND THE JAPANESE SOLDIER

To the Japanese soldiers and sailors the sight of *sake* (also known as *nihonshu*) could be the harbinger of good or bad news. For the Japanese soldier, the post-exchange (*Shuho*) was an important part of military life. It was there he could obtain cigarettes, towels, soap, toothpaste, stamps, postcards, noodles, and crackers. In addition to these items he could buy a bottle of *sake* for 10 *sen*, while a bottle of beer went for 18 *sen*. *Sake* was also distributed on the event of a holiday or the annual Regimental Color Celebration (*Gunkisai*). The site of *sake* could also be the bearer of an upcoming battle in which the men were not expected to survive.

"The taste of *sake* brings tears to my eyes because I can recall the many times I shared a final cup with my men sent on missions they would never return from." – Major Jiro Yoshida, Squadron Commander, 94 Sentai, Okinawa.

"Just prior to the invasion of Wake Island, our Captain ordered an *odaru* (barrel) of *sake* be broken open for us saying, 'I expect we will all perish in this battle.'" – Seaman 1st Class Hisao Tsuji, aboard the converted destroyer "Patrol Boat 33" after leaving Kwajalein to deliver Naval Landing Force troops against American-held Wake Island, December 23, 1941.[1]

"*Sake* was an indispensable item aboard our vessel, and was always available to us." – Petty Officer Goro Yamada, I-58 Submarine.

Solders smile at receiving a New Year's ration of *sake* and canned treats, January 2, 1938. (*Mainichi Shinbun*)

Tank crews exchange their parting cups at the battle of Imphal, Burma, 1944. (*Mainichi Shinbun*)

Warrant Officer Shigeru Fujii, 13th Independent mixed Regiment, travels through Kainan China atop a Type 94 scout tankette, February 10, 1939. (*Shigeru Fujii*)

Naval kamikaze pilots raising their cups in a final salute at takeoff, April 1945." Note the metal cups and the cherry blossoms placed in the helmet band of the pilot in the foreground. (*Mainichi Shinbun*)

"The supply unit brought up several large green bottles of *sake* for each tank platoon. I felt this would be my final taste of the homeland." Warrant Officer Shigeru Fujii (1st Tank Battalion, Independent Mixed 13th Regiment, IJA) describing his experience during the invasion of Hainan Island (China) February 10, 1938.[2]

Mr. Imashiro who served aboard the Cruiser *Yudachi* writes of beer, *sake* and even western wine being available for sale at the ship's canteen (*shuho*). He lamented that once en route to Kwajalein the ship had run out of *sake* so he consumed 'western wine' and experience the worst hangover to date. He also states that Petty Officers would often confiscate junior seaman's beer or *sake* and drink it themselves.

The people of Japan have a long tradition with the drinking of fermented rice wine known as "*Osake*". (The honorific "O" normally being added to show reverence, pronounced "*oh-saw-keh*", however in this book the honorific has been dropped)

Military leaders throughout history have known the importance of alcohol in boosting the courage of troops preparing for battle. Few in any country would argue against the ability of small amounts of alcohol to bolster a soldier's fighting spirit. However, to the Japanese soldier, the act of drinking *sake* transcended the physical reaction brought on by the absorption of alcohol into the bloodstream. The act of drinking *sake* was one of purification, of steeling the spirit for battle and of bidding farewell. Japanese soldiers would down a ceremonial cup of *sake* with the greeting, "*Yasukuni Jinji de Auo*" (I'll see you at the Yasukuni War Shrine). The fortified courage brought on by *sake* was more of an end result, and not entirely the ultimate goal of drinking *sake*. However, it must be said that Japanese soldiers were provided with regular beer and *sake* rations in the field even in front line conditions. Evidence is provided not only by Japanese and American veterans but by Japanese Army Quartermaster lists for the 28th Regiment "*Ichikitai*" that was wiped out by the U.S. 1st Marine Division at the battle of the Tenaru at Guadalcanal. The Regiment was issued a shipment of articles and supplies that included 5,000 liters of *sake*. This seems to be a lot of *sake* for roughly 900 men. However, after news of the Regiment's destruction the Japanese supply ship en route carrying the *sake* rations was diverted away.

Shattering the myth of the drunken Banzai attack? Japanese veterans have related they were conditioned from youth not to fear death. The shame of failing to fulfill one's duty was greater than losing one's life. For as the first precept of the Imperial Script reads, "Duty is heavier than a mountain, while

Army kamikaze pilots of the Hakko-tai unit, December 1944. (*Mainichi Shinbun*)

death is lighter than a goose down feather." (January 4, 1883).

Military men were educated by memorizing and reciting the Imperial precepts printed in red, making up the first twenty-eight pages of the soldiers ID booklet called "*Guntai Techo*". Within these pages are the five attributes of a soldier of the sun. These attributes often appear abbreviated on World War II *sake* cups:

- *Gunjin wa Chuusetsu* (A soldier is Loyal)
- *Gunjin wa Reigi* (A soldier is Polite)
- *Gunjin wa Buyu* (A soldier is Brave)
- *Gunjin wa Shingi* (A soldier is Trustworthy)
- *Gunjin wa Shiso* (A soldier is Thrifty)

(*see* page ____ for an example of a set of five cups combined to make this saying)

To understand the role of *sake* it must be understood the role of the soldier in Japan during the 1930s and 1940s. To the Japanese fighting man of World War II once he received his draft card, a pink postcard known as "*akagami*" (red card) he counted himself dead to his family. It was common for men to leave behind a short lock of hair and fingernail clippings for future burial should he fall on some foreign shore and never return. It was not a mere dramatic gesture, but a practical one that would ensure a proper cremation and Buddhist burial.

What World War II enthusiast hasn't heard urban legends of drunken kamikaze pilots being locked into the cockpit of their craft before takeoff? There is no evidence to suggest this idea of forced kamikaze attacks, while there are voluminous firsthand accounts to discredit this GI urban legend.

Japanese *kamikaze* pilots would share a parting cup of *sake* called "*Beppai*." There is a rare example of a ceremonial cup on display at the Tsuchiura base in Japan which was the location of the IJN Yokaren pilot training center. The cups were smashed after their contents were drunk.

A possible reason for the birth of this myth is that American servicemen had trouble grasping the notion of military suicide so the idea of being "drunk and locked in" was born. However, evidence proves not only were aviators eagerly giving their lives for the Emperor, they were doing so stone cold sober. One need only watch film footage taken during the April 1945 Kamikaze attacks that clearly show the skill displayed by Imperial Japanese Navy (IJN) pilots navigating their craft against U.S. vessels. Or to read accounts of Imperial Japanese Army (IJA) pilots who crashed their fighter aircraft into B-29's over Japan.

Evidence of battlefield beer and *sake* consumption is readily evident even today on far-flung pacific battlefields. Not only have Japanese IJN and IJA veterans related stories of battlefield consumption, but U.S. soldiers and Marines have also written and spoken of finding beer and *sake* bottles in abundance in caves and bunkers on many of the islands. Mr. Ivan Prall, former combat photographer on Iwo Jima related finding military motif *sake* bottles and *sake* cups on the island during the battle.[3] Former World War II 2nd Division Recon Marine Mr. Guy Gabaldon in his book *America Betrayed,* writes of finding beer, *sake*, rock candy, canned crab and lemon soda in the caves on Saipan during the war. He mentioned to the author of finding military *sake* cups in abundance on Saipan probably since the Japanese regiments had been recently sent there from China.[4] Finally, during his personal travels the author has seen firsthand evidence of beer and *sake* bottles in caves on Iwo Jima, Saipan, Peleliu, Guam, Chichi Jima, Wake Island, Guadalcanal, Thailand, Okinawa, Papua New Guinea and Rabaul.

With any subject there are varying accounts of *sake* use among different branches of the World War II Japanese armed forces. While some Japanese veterans account tales of free-flowing *sake* and beer available to both enlisted and officers alike, others inform that in their units *sake* was normally reserved for officers. In addition, it depended on the location of the unit as to whether there would be easy access to alcohol. Units station in the homelands (*naichi*) or in Korea or Manchuria would have much freer access to taverns, and bars that sold *sake*.

Former IJN Chief Petty Officer Goro Yamada told the author of being allowed to drink both beer and *sake* aboard the submarine *I-58*. There were no restrictions on either food or alcohol consumption, although severe consequences would be meted out for dereliction of duty, which was indeed rare. He spoke of witnessing a farewell salute with *sake* by the Kaiten suicide sub pilots aboard the *I-58* whose instruments of death came in the form mini-subs strapped to the deck of the larger submarine. Luckily for the eager suicide pilots the captain of the vessel Commander Mochitsura Hashimoto chose not to utilize the suicide *kaiten* torpedoes for the attack against the USS *Indianapolis*.[5]

Notes:

1 Phone interview with author 2002.
2 Personal interview in veteran's home in Gujohachiman, Gifu 1992.
3 Mr. S. Kajita 3rd Regiment Supply sated the *sake* cups in his unit were commemorative items made by the soldiers themselves as mementos for friends, family or employers (email correspondence with author 2002).
4 Ivan Prall (written correspondence 2002).
5 Guy Gabaldon (phone interview 2002).

3

MAKING A *SAKE* CUP

The word *sakazuki* comes from the reflection of the early evening moon reflected in the cups exchanged by ancient Japanese deities in a wedding ceremony. This mythical wedding between Prince *Oshihomimi* and Princess *Takuhatachichi* is credited with the familiar act of drinking partners exchanging cups of *sake* known as *tokomiki.*

Legend states the two deities exchanged scoops of the "ritual beverage" (*miki*) under blossoming peach trees. The male deity proffered the drink to the female. Then it was the male's turn to drink. After this, the two entered their chamber and again poured the drink for each other. They were now joined in the bond of love, and remained confined in the chamber for three days.

Sake cup store, circa 1905. (*Mainichi Shinbun*)

This is where the traditional Japanese wedding vows originate from, to commemorate the third day of the third month of the third year, the custom of *sansan-kudo* took shape."

The act of exchanging cups of *sake* between friends (*tokomiki*) is still very much the custom today in homes, restaurants and bars across Japan.

Guntai Sakazuki can be placed into one of three categories arranged here by order of commonality:

Ceramic
Lacquer
Metal

Ceramic *sake* cups

Yakimono are made from clay and fired in a kiln. The main points that were necessary for any kiln were the availability of supply of material suitable for making pottery, clay and wood. *Sake* cup clay is made of Kaolin which is found in granite areas, usually at the bottom of mountains. The other factor was the large volume of wood required to feed the kilns. A very zen-like Japanese approach to *sake* cup collecting is the fact that imperfections are appreciated. An imperfection proves the cup was made by hand under difficult circumstances. Cups produced today will not have flaws since they are fired with electric kilns that ensure constant heat control resulting in 'high quality' cups time after time. But with the traditional kilns craftsmen had to constantly keep the kilns stoked with Red Pine for one or two days straight and monitor the flame visually through years of practice. This is why *sake* cups made the traditional way (even with flaws) are more beautiful and possess an essence not found in the modern age of computers and mass-production. "*Yakimono*" consist of four types:

A. **Earthenware** (*Rakuyaki*) is a composition of blended clays, which harden depending on the intensity of the kiln. Due in part to their porous nature and fragility, Earthenware *sake* cups are very rare.

B. **Stoneware** is earthenware coated with a glaze consisting of a liquid paste made of feldspar rock powder mixed with ash (wood, straw, rice hull). When fired at great heat, the clay body becomes nonporous.

C. **Faience or half porcelain** (*Toki* or *hanjiki*) is made of kaolin clay which once glazed at lower temperature become hard. The color is not as bright and white as porcelain but is glassy and smooth. In general, the Japanese do not place as much importance on thin porcelain, as is often favored in Europe, which is why most Japanese ceramics can be classified as half porcelain; the shape, color (even imperfections), and overall appeal are the aspects that provide the most character.

D. **Porcelain** (*Jiki*) is of Chinese origin being produced by firing a pure clay called kaolin, which once glazed at high temperature (1400 degree) becomes hard, white, translucent and very glassy. Its hardness, ringing sound when struck, translucence, and gloss finish characterize it. This porcelain is also known as "China" or "Bone china" since it is comprised of 5% bone ash and china clay. Due to their detail and beauty, the most sought after *sake* cups tend to be of Kutani manufacture. Kutani cups are marked on the bottom, usually in red, with the *kanji* characters for "nine" (*Ku*) and "valley" (*Tani*).

The process used to manufacture Kutani ceramic can be separated in three main steps. The first one consists in preparing the clay to be used to shape the pottery. The pottery is formed using a potter wheel and is dried before being fired for eight hours at 800 degrees. The next and most important step is more specific to Kutani ceramics. A drawing is outlined on the cup with a cobalt pigment called *'Gosu'* then covered with glaze. After firing this turns into a sort of glass and is referred to as "Underglazing" (*sometsuke*). The cobalt pigment turns a deep blue color. This operation requires a firing temperature of 1300 degrees for fifteen hours. The temperature must remain constant throughout the firing process. One can easily understand that before the days of computer monitored electric or gas kilns the importance of the skill required to keep the flame at a constant temperature using nothing more than wood (only Japanese Red Pine *Akamatsu* is used, and charcoal.)

Many kilns produced plain white pottery to be painted by specialized kilns called *nishiki* kilns that were flourishing in the area surrounding Kanazawa at the turn of the century. After the glazing process begins the painting process that can cover several steps. In the traditional *Kutani* style there are only five colors used, purple, dark green, red, yellow and deep blue. There might be several paintings each requiring a firing between 800-1000 degrees. This operation is called Overglaze Painting or *Uwaestuke* or more generally *Iroestuke*. The last step is reserved for the gold or silver painting used to write the owner's information on the cup such as name or regiment. This step requires a final firing of 400 degrees.

Lacquer *sake* cups

These are carved from wood and brushed with layers of Japanese lacquer known as *nurushi*, giving the cups a plastic appearance. The cups are universally red, with a few rare examples in green. These cups are also known as "Japan," and were usually issued with a wooden box to protect the edges of the cup.

Metal *sake* cups

These are encountered in tin, silver, and combinations of metals. These are the hardest to find, yet often lack any personalization due to their nature of being formed in a mold. Metal cups, especially silver cups presented by the Emperor (*shihai*), were presented in wooden boxes fashioned from pawlonia (K*iri*) wood and are highly sought after, not only for their beauty, but also their historical significance.

4

SAKE BREWING

The people of Japan began producing *sake* sometime after the introduction of wet rice cultivation in the third century B.C. The first written record of *sake* being enjoyed in Japan dates from about 300 A.D. In ancient Japan, *sake* production and consumption was reserved primarily for the Imperial court, as well as large Buddhist temples and Shinto shrines. This is why *sake* is associated with religious rituals and festivals. Even today, *sake* is served at traditional ceremonies and weddings throughout Japan.

The ingredients of *sake* are rice and water interacting with microbes known as *koji* and *sake* yeast.

Japanese rice can be roughly classified into two varieties: the first is ordinary rice, which is used principally for eating; the second variety, *Sakamai*, is used exclusively for *sake* production. *Sakamai* not only features larger, softer grains than ordinary table rice, it is also more expensive, since it grows only in certain areas and requires more complex cultivation techniques. Although ordinary table rice can also be used to make *sake*, in general, *sake* made from *Sakamai* has a reputation for higher quality.

The water used in the production of *sake* is extremely important, because the mineral content of the water affects the taste. Semi-hard water is most suitable for *sake* production due to its lower iron and manganese content. Japan has a large amount of precipitation (approximately 1,500 mm/year) and ample high-quality ground water throughout the country. As a result, excellent *sake* can be produced in nearly every region.

Sake is at the same time a wine and a beer. Although *sake* is defined as a brewed alcoholic beverage, the brewing process is more complex than that employed for beer and wine. In the typical wine production process, the crushed grapes ferment naturally after yeast is added. In the case of beer, similarly, fermentation takes place after yeast and hot water are added to crushed malt. But the rice used to make *sake* does not begin to ferment with the addition of yeast alone. *Sake* brewing begins with the introduction of *koji*, which break down rice starch into glucose in a process known as "saccharification." Next, *sake* yeast is added and fermentation begins. This process, in which saccharification and fermentation take place in the same vat at the same time, is called "multiple parallel fermentation." This is a unique feature of *sake* brewing that distinguishes it from every other brewing process.

Koji are microbes, similar to these used in blue cheese production. Both Soy Sauce *(shoyu)* and soybean paste *(miso)* are also produced using similar beneficial microbes.

The longer fermentation process, which can be as much as three to four times that of wine, produces a wide variety of amino acids, giving *sake* a balanced, rounded taste and fresh flavor.

Due to the complex nature of brewing *sake*, each brewery has a brewmaster known as a *toji*. The *toji* manages not only the *sake* brewing process, but also the activities of his brewing team, including their work shifts and living arrangements. The Japanese believe that maintaining team spirit is essential to *sake* brewing.

The *toji* lives at the work site as long as he is in control of the brewing process. When he grows old, he appoints a hand-picked successor, to whom he has passed down his brewing know-how and techniques.

The question is often asked if *sake* should be consumed hot or cold? It is typically warmed before drinking, although room temperature is acceptable. The Japanese will often select the temperature of the *sake* depending on the season or the type of food one is partaking.

Compared with beer and wine, *sake* is drunk at a much wider range of temperatures, extending from approximately

Sake shop in Kyoto called Maizuruya, circa 1930. (*Gekkeikan, USA*)

5°-55°C (41°-131°F). It should not be heated above 60°C (140°F), though even if one wishes to drink hot *sake*, it's definitely not advisable to boil it.

Sake can be served at different temperatures each having its own name such as "hot" *(atsukan)*, "warm" (*nurukan*), or "lukewarm" *(hitohada)*. When it is served cold, *sake* at around fifteen degrees is known as "cool chilled" (*suzubie*), when chilled to ten degrees is called "flower chilled" *(hanabie),* and when chilled down to around five degrees is referred to as "cool chilled" (*yukibie*).

In the late *Meiji* Era (the early 20th century), Fukuoka Prefecture produced the smoothest *sake*. Its popularity exploded causing the industry to grow throughout the prefecture. It grew so well that Fukuoka became the second largest brewer in Japan during the 1940s, right behind Nara-led Hyogo Prefecture. For some reason, Fukuoka *sake* became popular as "battlefield *sake*" (*senba no sake*). This reputation began during the war with China in 1894, continued through the war with Russia in 1904, and held firm during World War II.[1]

Notes:

1 http://www.e*sake*.com/restructure/Knowledge/Newsletter/JT/JT2002/jt2002_17.html

Hamamatsu city musem webpage (7th Squadron)

http://peaceact.jca.apc.org/resources/noawacs_200204062.html

-Taiheiyou Sensou Rentai Rekishi (Jinbutsu Publishing)

-Japanese Military Uniforms 1930-1945 (Nainippon Eiga Publishing)

-Nihon Kaigun Gunkan Souran (Jinbutsu Publishing)

-Japanese English Character Dictionary (Tuttle)

-Handbook on Japanese Miliary Forces (U.S. War Dept Technical Manual TME-30-480 10/44-9/45)

5

COLLECTING

The field of *sake* cup collecting is so vast that readers are strongly urged to find an area of interest within the *sake* cup field and collect that variation – navy, aviation, armored vehicles, cavalry, home-leave, killed in action, discharge commemorative, home leave commemorative, entrance into the military commemorative, promotion commemorative, etc. – rather than try and collect "one of every type". It seems to be one of the few items of militaria that men and women share a common interest in.

There are those who collect based solely on aesthetic appeal, while others based on regimental history, still others collect *sake* trays or *sake* bottles. Fortunately, collecting cups has become easier with the advent of on-line auctions and catalogs such as "Ebay." There are several expatriots and servicemen living in Japan who visit the local antique dealers and flea markets looking for World War II memorabilia. These people often turn up nice *sake* cups for sale at affordable prices. The collector should avoid cups that are chipped, faded or have common scenes such as crossed flags or a plain star. It must be said that no matter how poor in quality a cup might appear it could still be a diamond in the rough! Two examples from the author's collection include a seemingly insignificant note "Kemptei Cup" (*see* page ___ for color photographs).

With regards to exactly which types of cups to collect, there are those who seek certain designs or motifs, while others collect based on theater of operations or unit designation. This is good news for beginners who do not want to spend a lot of money at the outset of the hobby. Due to the time and effort needed to kiln and paint a *sake* cup there are no replicas on the market. Even a beginner can assemble an impressive collec-

tion without fear of getting stung by reproductions. The same cannot be said of most other fields of collecting.

In regards to condition, the following is a basic guide to condition codes. However, before buying any cup it is important to ask questions regarding its condition and not assume the item is in good shape: *Poor Condition* – The colors and inscription are faded and the cup is chipped or cracked in more than one place; *Good Condition* – The colors have some fading possible minor chip to the edge or a hairline crack; *Excellent Condition* – No fading, no chips or cracks; *Mint Condition* – Pristine with high luster and no damage. It is advisable to always collect high quality items unless the item itself is of such a rare nature that some amount of damage can be overlooked. It should be pointed out that it is indeed a mystery as to how many of the cups survived the horrendous bombings brought upon Japan during 1945. Most of Japan's major cities were reduced by 25%-75% and some were completely demolished, yet somehow these beautiful cups miraculously survive.

6

VALUE

The author has watched the price of *sake* cups rise over the past decade, and there is little on the horizon to indicate the price of them dropping. Where else can one obtain, for the price of dinner, an authentic World War II or pre-World War II piece of history?

There are three basic factors that determine a cup's worth or value. These same guidelines apply to *sake* bottles and *sake* trays:

1. **Design** – Is the design attractive, are the colors bright, and is the artwork done well? Does it have an airplane or a tank, or is it just crossed flags and a star? A cup with a vehicle (truck, tank, or ship) will demand a higher asking price, while a cup with a badge or medal would garnish an even higher asking price.

2. **Unit** – Is the cup from a well-known regiment? Is the cup for a supply clerk or a pilot, an enlisted man or an officer?

3. **Condition** – Are there any chips or cracks, and is the artwork scratched or faded? While many Westerners show disdain for a bulge or flaw, it is these naturally occurring kiln flaws that give each cup its personality and should increase value.

4. **Material** – Is the cup made from porcelain, lacquerware, or metal? Metal cups, especially silver, will bring a higher price.

Thanks in part to the internet, the interest in World War II Japan has risen over the years, bringing the average price of cups to $25, with prices often reaching the $60+ level regularly. Sadly, it is regrettable that several years from now readers will look back and long for the "good old days" when a *sake* cup could be bought for $20-$30. As with all things collectable, with increased popularity comes increased prices.

Sake trays currently range in the $40-$100 range depending on artwork and condition. *Sake* bottle prices range from $40-$200, also depending on artwork and condition. Ultra rare and unusual *sake* bottles, such as the whistling bottles and the three-piece bottles with a separate bullet shell cap and base, are always sought after. Generally, the cups are easiest to find, then bottles, and finally the *sake* trays.

Collectors often speak of looking for *kutani sake* cups. The process of making these colored, bone-china cups in the village of Kutani dates back to the middle of the 17th century when, as part of a government policy to encourage local industry (and the fact that high-quality clay was discovered there), a kiln to make colored porcelain was established at the village (now in present day Ishikawa Prefecture). Skilled potters were brought from Hizen (in present-day Saga Prefecture), which was known at the time as a center of porcelain production. This was the beginning of the local manufacture of colored china.

This type of pottery was naturally named *Kutani-yaki* after the village where it began, and had a distinctive style that involved plentiful use of *Kutani gosai*, or the five hues of Kutani – including deep blue, purple, yellow, green, and red – which were used to cover the entire surface with colored decoration. Themes included birds and flowers, landscape motifs, and geometrical patterns.

7

PRE-WORLD WAR II

1894-1895 Sino-Japanese War (*Nisshin Senso*)
China's defeat demonstrated the success of early Meiji "strengthening" modernization policies. Taiwan was ceded to Japan as war reparations. The defeat of China sparked a scramble for concessions among foreign powers eager to carve up China. Tension increased between Russia and Japan over mutual concerns regarding Korea and Manchuria.

1904-05 Russo-Japan War (*Nichiro Senso*)
Prior to war with Russia, Japan had forged an alliance with Great Britain in 1902. This move had strengthened Japan's position vis-a-vis Russia. Any nation attacking Japan would also have to face the British who had the world's most formidable navy. Japan established southern Manchuria as its sphere of influence in China and embarked on huge overseas investment. Korea was annexed in all but name.

The turn of the century was a time when nations jostled for territory and trade. The Russo-Japanese War of 1904-1905 was waged mainly for the control of Manchuria and Korea. The U.S. supported Japan and hoped she would keep Korea open to all nations for commerce. The war started before a formal declaration with Japan launching a surprise attack to destroy part of the Russian fleet at Port Arthur in Manchuria and landing troops in Korea. Great Britain and U.S. assumed Japan would open up trade in Asian markets. President Theodore Roosevelt is reported to have feared that if Japan won the war, there might be a struggle between the U.S. and Japan in the future. This battle was significant in that it was the first in which an Asian nation, Japan, defeated a European power.

In the famous Battle of the Sea of Japan (Tsushima) on May 27-28, 1905, Japan defeated the Russian fleet, which had sailed from the Baltic Sea eighteen months before. Even before this battle, Japan was financially drained and asked Roosevelt to mediate an end to the war. Although Japan was winning the war, they were heavily outnumbered. The Russian czar, however, finally relented after seeing his Baltic fleet destroyed. It was during this war that Japan's army headed by Maresuke Nogi attacked 203-Meter Hill (*nihyakusan kouchi*) suffering horrendous losses but taking the hill in what would be prophetic bayonet charges.

A peace conference attended by President Theodore Roosevelt was held at Portsmouth, New Hampshire in July and August 1905.

It is hard to fathom the fact the Japanese soldiers and sailors who took on the Russian nation had they themselves been the offspring of men who had served as samurai merely a generation before! The fathers of the Russo-Japan war veterans had lived in a feudal country that was only then slowly emerging from a position of closed doors to openly embracing Western ideas.

1918-1922 Siberian Expedition (*Saibiria Shuppei*)
During and after World War I, with the "Siberian Intervention" Japan launched a large-scale effort to expand its influence over Siberia and the Russian Far East, enlarge its colonial empire by whatever means and thus reduce Russian influence in East Asia.

1914-1918 World War I (*Dai ichi sekai taisen*)
Seizing the opportunity of Berlin's distraction with the European War and wanting to expand its sphere of influence in China, Japan declared war on Germany in August 1914 and quickly occupied German-leased territories in China's Shandong Province and the in the Pacific islands of the Marianas, Carolines, and Marshall islands. With its Western allies heavily involved in the war in Europe, Japan sought further to consolidate its position in China by presenting the Twenty-One Demands to China in January 1915. Besides expanding its control over the German holdings, Japan sought joint ownership of a major mining and metallurgical complex in central China, prohibitions on China leasing any coastal areas to a third power, which, if achieved, would have reduced China to a Japanese protectorate. In the face of slow negotiations with the Chinese government, widespread anti-Japanese sentiments in China, and international condemnation, Japan withdrew the last set of demands, and treaties were signed in May 1915.

Japan's power in Asia grew with the demise of the tsarist regime in Russia and the disorder wrought in 1917 by the Bolshevik Revolution. Wanting to seize the opportunity, the Japanese army planned to occupy Siberia as far west as Lake Baykal. To do so, Japan had to negotiate an agreement with China allowing the transit of Japanese troops through Chinese territory. Although the force was scaled back to avoid antagonizing the United States, more than 70,000 Japanese troops joined as an Ally to the much smaller units of the Allied Expeditionary Force sent to Siberia in 1918.

8

WORLD WAR II

Most Westerners view World War II as beginning on 7:55am Sunday, December 7, 1941, on Oahu island Territory of Hawaii. While this is true, it can be said that World War II actually began some ten years earlier when the Japanese invaded Shanghai in her attempt to broaden her borders and increase agricultural area.

In fact, the Japanese view World War II as two separate yet entwined wars: the China Incident, which lasted from 1931-1945, and the Pacific War, lasting from 1941-1945. Oddly, the Japanese today commonly believe that although they were largely to blame for their transgression into China, they are only partly to blame for the Pacific War. It is widely held opinion in Japan that during the early part of the 20th century Western nations held a double standard regarding their own overseas expansion against the plans of Japan.

It should also be mentioned that just barely eighty years prior to the outbreak of World War II the feudal nation of Japan was grudgingly opening its doors to Western influence, and in an admirably short span of time went from a third world nation to one that would openly challenge a large portion of the world's entire population!

Head naval officers celebrate the news of the Pearl Harbor attack, Osaka, December 1941. (*Mainichi Shinbun*)

1931-1945 China Incident, Shanghai Expedition, Tienshin Mukden, Korea, Taiwan

September 18 Manchurian Incident: Japan takes over Northeast China and sets up the puppet state Manchukuo. July 7, 1937, outbreak of the second Sino-Japanese War. Japan occupies east and central China.

1941-1945 Co-prosperity Sphere of Influence War *Daitoa Senso*, Pacific War

Japan's leaders played upon centuries of ill feelings between Asians and their European "masters" and created the self-governing freedom plan known as "Asia for the Asians." Needless to say, this plan should have been labeled "Asia for the Japanese," since the only country truly benefiting from the alliance was Japan.

President Roosevelt and Secretary of State Cordell Hull shut off American supplies in an effort to force the Japanese to end hostilities against China. The Japanese had long coveted the resource-rich British and Dutch colonies of Southeast Asia, and as the U.S. trade embargo tightened, the Japanese increasingly looked southward for raw materials and strategic resources.

The U.S. Pacific Fleet at Pearl Harbor was the only force capable of challenging Japan's navy, and American bases in the Philippines could threaten lines of communication between the Japanese home islands and the East Indies. Every oil tanker heading for Japan would have to pass by American-held Luzon. From these needs and constraints, Japan's war plans quickly emerged.

Japan prepared a repeat performance of an undeclared first strike against a Western power's navy with the Pearl Harbor attack. The plan was to neutralize the American fleet and seize America's central Pacific bases at Guam and Wake islands and invade the Philippines. With American naval power crippled, Japan's military would be free to seize Burma, Malaya, Singapore, and the Dutch East Indies in a series of rapid amphibious operations. Japan would then establish a defensive ring around its newly conquered empire by fortifying islands in the south and the central Pacific.

General army and naval officers exchange *sake* celebrating the fall of Hankow, China, at the Hankow Palace Hotel, August 1940. (*Mainichi Shinbun*)

Japan's leaders were convinced that Americans, once involved in the European war, would be quick to negotiate peace in the Pacific.

The Japanese war plan worked like clockwork. On December 7, 1941, Japan paralyzed the Pacific Fleet in its attack on Pearl Harbor. In the Philippines, Japanese fliers destroyed most of MacArthur's air force on the ground. Freed of effective opposition, Japanese forces marched through the pro-Japanese nation of Thailand to take Burma, Malaya, Singapore, and the Dutch East Indies in rapid succession. By March 1942, the Japanese had conquered an empire. Only MacArthur's beleaguered American-Filipino army still held out on the main Philippine island of Luzon.

However, within five months the last of the organized Philippine military defenders had surrendered. By May 1942, the Philippine resistance had ended. The Japanese had succeeded beyond their wildest expectations. A vast new empire had fallen into their hands at so little cost, which tempted them further. If their forces could move into the Solomon Islands and the southern coast of New Guinea, they could threaten Australia and cut the American line of communications to MacArthur's base there. If they could occupy Midway Island, only 1,000 miles from Honolulu, they could force the American fleet to pull back to the west coast. In Japanese overconfidence lay the seeds of Japan's first major defeats.

Many Japanese soldiers who had experienced victories in China were later sent to the graveyards of the Pacific, from whence there would be no more "triumphant return." *Sake* cups from the Pacific War are perhaps rarest of them all. We see no commemorative home leave cups, no discharge *sake* cups, etc., only the standardized "Greater East Asia Co-Prosperity Sphere War" on these cups. The soldiers and sailors were to be destroyed on the likes of battlefields such as Peleliu, Saipan, Iwo Jima, the Philippines, and Okinawa. The estimated number of Japanese servicemen killed in World War II is roughly 3,000,000.

10

MISCELLANEOUS *SAKE* CUPS

Helmet cups

Helmet cups are very popular with *sake* cup collectors due to the fact they can be viewed and enjoyed either upright or upside down. The helmet cups resemble the standard Model 90 Japanese Army/Navy steel combat helmet (*tetsu kabuto*), complete with a star and rivets. Oddly, the navy helmet cups feature a blossom instead of an anchor on the front of the cup. Helmet cups usually command double the price of a standard *sake* cup when the artwork is equal. In addition to helmet cups there are also the very rare "combat cap cups" and "peaked cap cups," with all the complete chinstraps, ventholes, and buttons. These latter are even more desirable and should be purchased if encountered for $75 or less.

Other

There are many one-of-a-kind cups that do not neatly fall into a particular category, such as a "Death in battle" cup, a "*Kempeitai*" cup, or an "Imperial Guard Cup."

Imperial Guard *sake* cups are also an interesting area of collecting, since they provide the oldest links to the Emperor. In 1875 the 1st Imperial Guard Regiment was organized at the palace to provide direct protection for the Emperor. At that

1st Imperial Guard regimental color ceremony, 1938. Note the *sake* barrel. (*Chuck Waud*)

time there were many factions of disgruntled samurai *(bushi)* in the areas around Tokyo, Sendai, Nagoya, Osaka, Hiroshima, and Kumamoto, giving rise to fears for the Emperor's safety. Soon after, the members of the elite Guard were taken from the best of the Japanese regiments across Japan. However, the Imperial Guards Regiments 1, 2, 3, and 4 grew to full combat readiness and saw extensive action in all of Japan's conflicts.

The Imperial Guards were massed at the Taisho Emperor's enthronement in Kyoto held in 1915, as well as at the Showa Emperor's enthronement in Kyoto, November 1928.

The Imperial Guards were also present at the celebration of the 2600th anniversary of the Imperial household reign on February 9, 1940. One can find *sake* cups with this commemorative but they are rare. Attendees to the event were on official duty or were invited via special engraved invitation. The author has one such invitation, along with a medal, award document, and *sake* cup in his collection. They are indeed rare.

The Imperial Guard was also at the Emperor's side as he reviewed the annual large scale war games held in Japan *(Rikugun Tokubetsu Dai Enshu)*.

With the adoption of the Japanese Constitution (*Kempo*) in 1890 (Meiji year 22) the Japanese instituted a universal military draft (*Chouhei*) encompassing men from the ages of 17-40 (In 1943 the age was raised to 45). Once called upon, soldiers would serve in the standing army for three years, then serve in the Reserves for four years, four months, and conclude their service with another five years in the secondary Reserves. This resulted in a period of twelve plus years of compulsory military service. It should be noted this was in addition to the military education and training boys received in Primary and Secondary Schools. This helps to explain the tenaciousness of the Japanese fighting man, who had come from a culture of military discipline.

In March 1941 a Japanese Infantry Division (10,000) consisted of three Regiments, with each Regiment consisting of a Regimental Headquarter, three Infantry Battalions with corresponding Headquarters, four Companies, a Machine Gun Company, a Field Artillery Battalion, a Field Artillery Battalion Headquarters, a Field Artillery Company, and a Communications Company. Each Regiment within the Division was naturally equipped with Type 38 Arisaka Rifles and complimented with the following weapons: Type 41 Mountain Gun (4); Type 92 Infantry Gun (6); Type 94 37mm Gun (4); Type 97 Automatic Gun (6); Type 92 Heavy Machine Gun (24); and the Type 11 Light Machine Gun (108).

Since the majority of military *sake* cups were produced prior to the outbreak of the Pacific war it is easy to understand why most weapons that are featured on *sake* cups are from the pre-1941 Regimental weapons table of organization. The author has never encountered later war weapons, such as the Type 99 Light Machine gun or the Type 89 Grenade Discharger (Knee mortar) on a *sake* cup, bottle, or tray.

Navy Cups

Navy *sake* cups are sought after by collectors for their rarity. To begin with, the number of sailors versus soldiers was disproportionate, creating a built-in difference in the number of navy veterans versus army veterans creating *sake* cups. This can be said of all areas of Japanese World War II militaria collecting. Anything "navy" will fetch a higher price due to its rarity. Of interest is the fact that most naval *sake* cups will universally feature a crane and turtle or cherry blossoms. The Japanese have a saying that "A crane lives 1,000 years, a turtle lives 10,000 years" (*tsuru wa sennen, kame wa mannen*). Naval cups will usually bear the inscription for "term fulfillment discharge,"—not the usual regimental numbers as is commonly encountered on Army cups—thus making identification to a particular unit impossible. Occasionally a naval cup will bear the inscription of the ship's name, but these cups are indeed rare.

When checking Naval *sake* cups one will find poetic names bestowed on these seagoing vessels of death, which is characteristic of the Japanese moral aestheticism that made "war and death" things of beauty.

Japanese destroyers were named after phenomena of weather, sky, and sea, with several groups based on the elements of wind (*kaze*), snow (*yuki*), rain (*ame*), clouds (*kumo*), waves (*nami*), mist (*kiri*), frost (*shimo*), tides (*shio*), and moons (*tsuki*).

Capital ships were mostly named after provinces, although *Kongo*-class, being battlecruisers, were named after mountains. Aircraft carriers and seaplane carriers were usually named after mythical flying creatures. Heavy Cruisers were named mostly after mountains, but *Mogami*-class were named after rivers. Light cruisers were generally named after rivers and streams. First class destroyers were named after environmental or calendar names. Second-class destroyers were named after plants.

Naval Landing Force officers raise glasses to commemorate a victory over Chinese forces, October 1937. (*Mainichi Shinbun*)

11

JAPANESE LANGUAGE AND *KANJI*

As most readers have already surmised, the Japanese language is not an easy one to master. The Japanese written language consists of three different alphabets: *Hirgana* (52 letters); *Katakana* (52 letters); and *Kanji* (3,000+ characters). While *Hiragana* and *Katakana* can be learned in a week of concerted study, the third alphabet of *Kanji* takes years of serious dedication. The Japanese themselves learn *Kanji* from the first grade through the twelfth grade. First year students only learn the first 46 *kanji*, with successive years bringing more *kanji*; the students study and memorize until they have conquered all 1,850 of the standardized *Toyo Kanji* as laid out by the Japanese Ministry of Education.

In order to read Japanese, one must be able to recognize all three alphabets and how they interact with one another. Luckily, neither the *Hiragana* nor *Katakana* change pronunciation when combined with other characters; however, the same cannot be said for *Kanji*, whose pronunciation will change. For example, the character "live" can be pronounced several different ways: *u*, *ki*, *nama*, *i*, *iki*, *sei*, and *sho* retaining the general meaning; *Umare kokyo* (*u*) Place of birth; *Kiippon* (*ki*) Pure; *Namamizu* (*nama*) Unboiled water; *Seiniku* (*sei*) Fresh meat; *Ikijigoku* (*iki*) Living Hell; *Seizonsha* (*Sei*) Survivor; and *Shogai* (*sho*) Suicide. Luckily, the *sake* cup collector need not worry about learning all of these different variations. There are basically a few dozen different phrases on Japanese military *sake* cups.

Due to different artists' handwriting styles it is impossible to list examples of all variations of characters. Artists would use signature swirls and abbreviate the *kanji* for aesthetic beauty. With some practice, the collector can identify the cups in his collection using the *kanji* tables provided at the end of this chapter.

It should be noted that the characters on the very bottom of the cup are those of the kiln, or more commonly the artist, while a name appearing inside the cup belongs to the owner.

English on *sake* cups

Very rarely one will encounter English on *sake* cups. However, examples do exist. While on regular cups the Japanese writing went from RIGHT to LEFT prior to and during World War II, those cups with English on them are written "backwards" from LEFT to RIGHT! These international English symbols were used by the Japanese military prior to and during World War II and would have been very familiar to the fighting man. Here are some examples:

Machine Gun squad leader Yoshiyuki Morikwaki, 1939. Note the "MG" armband. (*Yoshiyuki Moriwaki*)

Army

I	Infantry Regiment (*Hohei Rentai*)
HA	Anti AA (*Kosha ho*)
K	cavalry (*Kihei*)
KB	Cavalry brigade (*Kihei Ryodan*)
KI	Balloon unit (*Kikyutai*)
LM	Light trench mortar unit (*Keihakugekihotai*)
MG	Machine Gun Unit (*Kikanju tai*)
NW	Grenadier discharger/rifle (*Kikidanto kikidanju*)
PA	Mechanized army (*Kikogun*)
PS	Independent engineer (*Dokuritsu Kohai*)
PT	Carrier pigeon (*Hatotai Shikyutai*)
PW	Tankette unit (*Sokosha Heitai*)
S	March causalities collecting unit (*Kanja shuyotai*)
SA	Medium artillery (*Yasen Juhohei*)
SAM	Medium artillery (*Yasen Juho Danyaku*)
SAS	Independent medium artillery (*Dokuritsu Yasen Juhohei*)
RD	Special radio unit (*Tokushu Musentai*)
TD	Armored division (*Sensha Shidan*)
VR	Veterinary (*Juizairyo*)
Z	Gas (*Gasubutai*)

Navy

SG	Sub Group (*Sensu Suitai*)
CS	Cruiser division (*Junyokan Sentai*)
DF	Aircraft carrier (*Kokubokan*)
BS	Battleship Divsion (*Senkan Sentai*)
FB	Naval Air Force (*Kokubutai*)
LG	Special Naval Landing Force (*Tokubetsu Rikusentai*)
NG	Night combat unit (*Yasentai*)
BG	Naval defense force (*Bobitai*)
HG	Heavy gun unit (*Juhotai*)

The author has seen *sake* cups in collections in Japan, the U.S., and Australia that have English unit abbreviations and owners' names. These are cups produced about the turn of the century when Japan was enamored with Western culture and science.

Conclusion

Japanese Military *sake* cup collecting spans a period of sixty years of Japanese overseas expansion. They are affordable, interesting and definitely rising in value.

NUMBERS

1st
一代

2nd
二代

3rd
三代

4th
四代

5th
五代

6th
六代

7th
七代

8th
八代

9th
九代

10th
十代

UNITS

Squad
隊分

Platoon
隊小

Company
隊中

Regiment
隊連

Battalion
隊大

Division
団師

Army
軍陸

Navy
軍海

Kanto Army
軍東関

VEHICLES

Ship
艦軍

Warship
艦戦

Cruiser
艦逐駆

Destroyer
艦洋巡

Aircraft Carrier
艦母空航

Airplane
機行飛

Tank
車戦

Truck/Car
車動自

Artillery
砲大

Field Artillery
砲戦野

Mountain Artillery
砲山

Machine Gun
銃関機

Anti-Aircraft
砲射高

PLACES

Japan
本日

China
那支

Korea
鮮朝

Russia
露

Manchuria
州満

Northern Manchuria
州満北

Southern Manchuria
州満南

Taiwan
湾台

Siberia
亜利伯西

Hong Kong
港香

Singapore
港星

Mukden
天奉

Port Arthur
順旅

Dairen
連大

Peking
京北

JAPANESE IMPERIAL REIGNS

Meiji 1868 - 1912
治明

Taisho 1915 - 1926
正大

Showa 1926 - 1989
和昭

CONFLICTS

Sino-Japan War
争戦清日

Russo-Japan War
争戦露日

Siberia Conflict
変事亜利伯西

China Incident
変事那支

Pacific War
争戦亜東大

Holy War
戦聖

RANKS
(ARMY)

Private 2nd Class
兵等二

Private 1st Class
兵等一

Supior Private
兵等上

Staff Lance Corporal
長兵

Corporal
長伍

Sergeant
曹軍

Sergeant Major
長曹

Cadet
生補侯部幹

Warrant Officer
尉准

2nd Lieutenant
尉少

1st Lieutenant
尉中

Captain
尉大

Major
佐少

Lieutenant Colonel
佐中

Colonel
佐大

Major General
将少

Lieutenant General
将中

General
将大

RANKS (NAVY)

Seaman
兵水等一

Able Seaman
兵水等上

Leading Seaman 2nd Class
長水兵

Leading Seaman 1st Class
兵水等上

Petty Officer 2nd Class
曹水兵等二

Petty Officer 1st Class
曹水兵等一

Chief Petty Officer
曹兵水等上

Warrant Officer
官士准

Ensign
尉少

Sub Lieutenant
尉中

Lieutenant
尉大

Lieutenant Commander
佐少

Commander
佐中

Captain
佐大

Rear Admiral
将少

Vice Admiral
将中

Admiral
将大

Company Grade Officer
官尉

Field Grade Officer
官左

General Officer
官将

SERVICE BRANCHES

Headquarters
部本

Infantry
兵歩

Cavalry
兵歩

Supply
重軸

Medical
生衛

Imperial Guard
衛近

Combat Engineer
作工

Communications
信電

FIVE IMPERIAL TEACHINGS FOR THE SOLDIERS
義教大五

A Soldier is Loyal

忠節は人軍

A Soldier is Polite

儀礼は人軍

A Soldier is Brave

勇武は人軍

A Soldier is Trustworthy

義信は人軍

A Soldier is Thrifty

素質は人軍

EVENTS

Emperor's Enthronement
念記典大御

Shooting Award
念記表撃射

Award
賞

Celebration
祝

Commemorative
念記

Entrance into Military
念記隊入

Home Leave
念記帰休

Dispatch
念記遣派

Discharge Commemorative
念記隊除
念記営退

Disband Commemorative
念記体解

Term Fulfillment Commemorative
念記期満
んねききんま

Reservist
人軍郷在

Victorious Return
念記旋凱

Off to War
念記征出

Red Cross Society
社字十赤

Kutani (*Sake* cup manufacturer)
谷九

COLOR PLATES

1898 - 1932

Banzai Imperial Forces, Victorious Army, 1898. $45

Woodblock print showing Japanese fighting Chinese, 1898. $75

The Fall of Mukden (Korea), 1898. $45

Victorious return commemorative, Shantung (China), 1917. In World War I the Japanese took over German concessions in Shantung by force. $45

Japanese 18th Infantry Regiment under Colonel Sato. $35

日本帝國明治三十七八年從軍記章之證
陸軍步兵一等卒 美馬萬太郎
明治三十七八年從軍記章條例ニ依リ
陸軍大臣ノ奏請ヲ經テ明治三十九年三月三十日
勅定ノ從軍記章ヲ授與ス
明治三十九年四月一日
奉勅
賞勲局總裁從二位勲一等子爵大給恒
此證ヲ勘査シ第 四萬五四壹八 號ヲ以テ
明治三十七八年從軍記章簿冊ニ登記ス
賞勲局書記官從四位勲三等橫田香苗
賞勲局書記官正六位勲五等藤井善言

Russo-Japanese war campaign medal awarded to 1st Private Mima, April 1, 1906. $65

天佑ヲ保有シ萬世一系ノ帝祚ヲ踐タル
日本國皇帝陸軍歩兵少佐従六位勲五等功五級小島鎰三郎
ヲ明治勲章ノ勲四等ニ敘シ瑞寶章ヲ
授與ス即チ此位ニ屬スル禮遇及ヒ特權
ヲ有セシム
神武天皇即位紀元二千五百六十四年
明治三十七年十一月廿九日東京帝宮ニ於テ
璽ヲ鈐セシム
賞勲局總裁従二位勲一等子爵大給恒
此證ヲ勘査シ第九万六千十九
號ヲ以テ勲等簿冊ニ記入ス
賞勲局書記官従四位勲三等横田香苗
賞勲局書記官正六位勲五等藤井善言

Russo-Japanese war award, Sacred Treasure 4th class Major Kojima, November 19, 1905. $125

Colonel Yamaguchi (right) commander of the 33rd Regiment consults with his officers in China, May 21, 1938. (*Mainichi Shinbun*)

Above: Russo-Japanese war veterans pay a visit to China Incident army soldiers, 1940. (*Shashin Shuho*)

Off to the Russo-Japanese war commemorative. Note the almost comical manner in which the Japanese soldier has grabbed the Russian soldier by the scruff of the neck, demonstrating a total disdain for the Russian man's fighting ability. $45

Above: Woodblock print of the Russo-Japanese war's most infamous battle, Tsushima Straights, which was fought between the Japanese combined fleet and the Russian Baltic Fleet on May 27, 1905. It was at this battle that Admiral Heihachiro Togo shattered the myth of European invincibility with the defeat of the Russian fleet. Admiral Togo's flagship was damaged, but was later rebuilt to its former glory as a floating museum in Yokosuka, Japan. It is the only surviving pre-dreadnought battleship in the world. $20

Celebration, the fall of Port Arthur. On February 8, 1904 the Japanese fleet made a surprise attack on the Russian Baltic fleet anchored at Port Arthur. After several failed relief attempts, the city of Port Arthur fell to the Japanese in February 1905. $30

Left: Off to Russo-Japanese war commemorative. $20

Below: Russo-Japanese war era artillery cups. Of note is the 28cm howitzer used effectively at the battle of Port Arthur.

Right: Commemorative of deeds during Russo-Japanese war, 1904-1905.

Below: Six cups form the Russo-Japanese war of 1905. Of note is the center cup at bottom showing the main gate of the 1st Imperial Guard Regiment that was founded in Meiji 7 (1875). $40

Above: Five "triumphant return" cups from the battle for Siberia, 1918-1922. $20 Below: Six cups from the Russo-Japanese war. Note the tattered regimental flag at top center. $20

Above: Boxed commemorative, 1905.
$25

Very rare cups with photos: top left, 19th Regiment Discharge; top right, Russo-Japanese war commemorative; bottom left, War God Nagase; bottom right, Admiral Heihachiro Togo.
$65

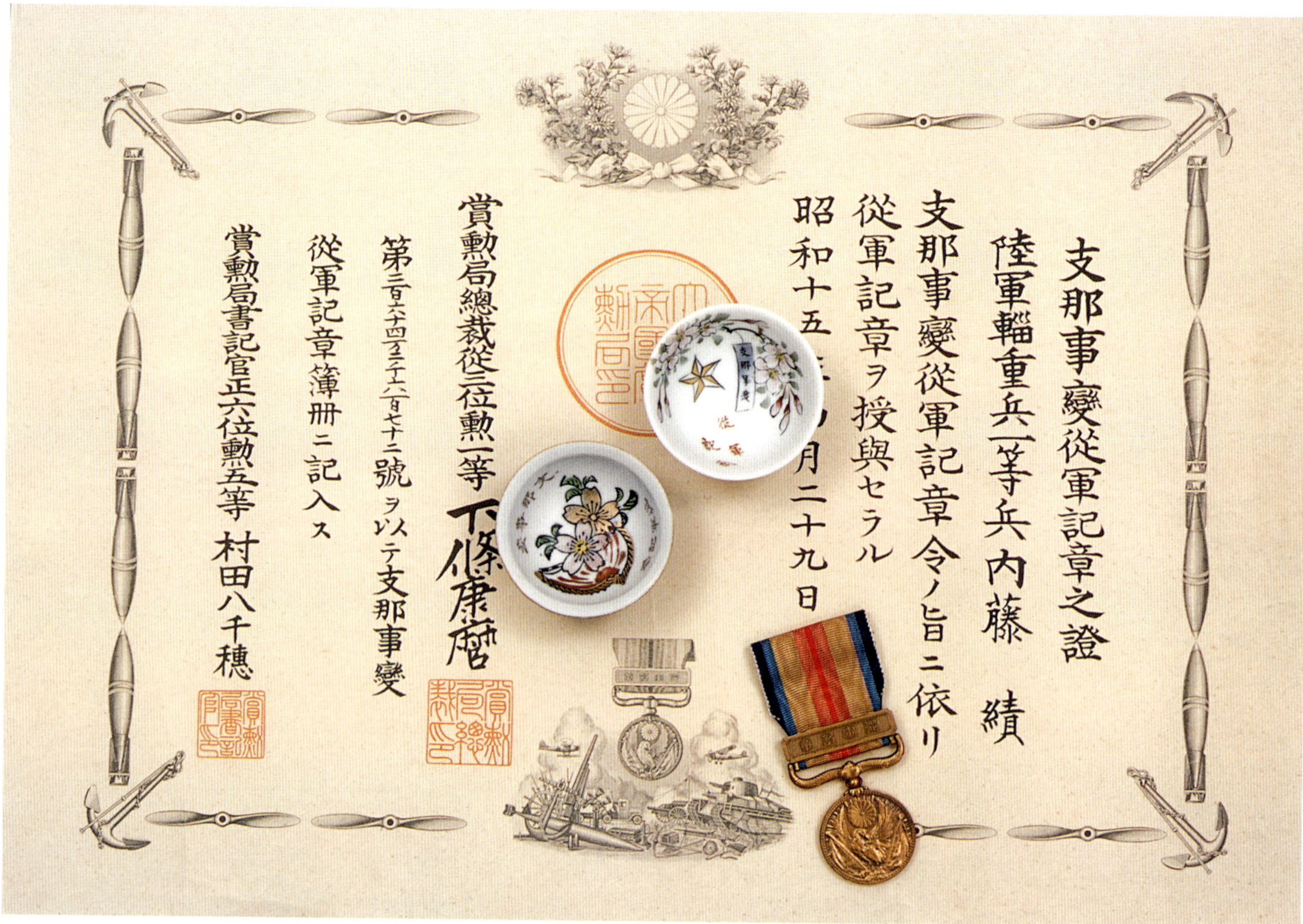

Above: China Incident Campaign medal award document with corresponding medal and cups. Document, $75. Cups, $25. Medal, $45

Victorious return commemorative, dispatch to Shinshu. Note the crossed Japanese and Manchurian flags. The *Manchukuo* flag's yellow field represents unification while the four colored bands stand for: bravery (red), justice (blue), purity (white) and determination (black). The puppet nation of *Manchukuo* existed in northeast China between 1932 and 1945 under the rule of the last Chinese emperor Puyi. $20

Shooting badge award and cup named to 2nd Class Private Mori of the 19th Infantry Regiment, dated August 10, 1920. Award, $75. Cup, $60

Various shooting badges. $40-$65

1932 - 1935

Left: U.S. and Japanese sailors in Shanghai on pre-war friendly terms, in 1937. Note the switched caps and uniforms! (*Author's collection*)

Below: Various china incident and Manchuria cups. Note the Great Wall of China. $20-$35

Original caption in German reads, "*Japanische Soldaten in Nordchina auf posten an der Chinesischen Mauer 28.4.44.*" (Japanese soldiers in north China on post at the Chinese wall 28.4.44.) Note the Japanese soldier standing guard at the Great Wall. (*Transocean Europapress*)

Above: Rare *sake* cups with human figures. All are from the China Incident. $35-$50

Japanese soldier places flowers and *sake* at his comrades graves shortly after the battle for Singapore, 1942. *Sake* was not only consumed during weddings, parties, ceremonies, and festivals, but was also commonly offered to the dead. (*Shashin Shuho*)

Right: Soldier in front of a map of China. China Incident Victory Commemorative. The cities named are Shanghai, Nanking, Tienshin, and Peking. $35

Below: Battle in the streets of China, 1939. Note the Type 89 grenade discharger, commonly referred to as the "knee mortar." Hard won victories were the subject for most *sake* cups. (*Shashin Shuho*)

Soldiers share a victory cup of *sake* in China, 1938. (*Shashin Shuho*)

Discharge commemorative, China Incident. This is a *kutani* cup as can be ascertained by the elaborate design and distinctive colors.

Various *sake* cups with regimental flash collar insignia. (*tachi eri sho*). The Japanese army changed from stand-up collar insignia to collar tab insignia in 1938, which dates these cups between 1930-1938. Collecting by regiment can be interesting as well. $25-$35

Transport *sake* cups from the 3rd and 4th supply units. Cups with vehicles on them are very rare and highly sought after. $50

Above: Medical *sake* cups. $30-$40

Army medical unit, draft commemorative. $30

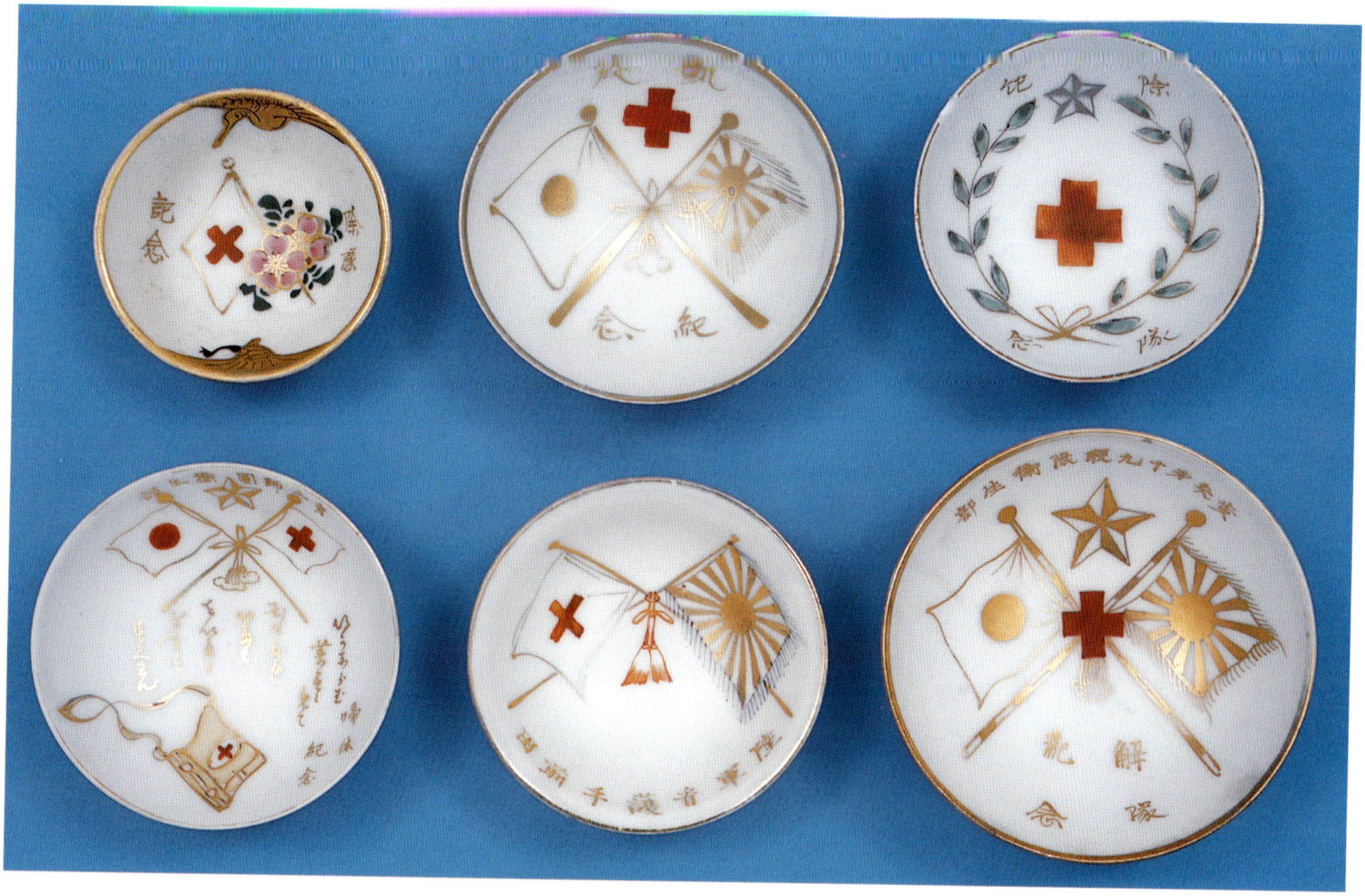

Above: Various medical *sake* cups. Note that the bottom center cup is for an Army nurse, and the medical bag on lower left cup. $30-$40 Right: Army nurse partaking of "God sake" (*Shinshu*), prior to entering the front line, 1943. (*Mainichi Shinbun*)

Various Shanghai incident *sake* cups. On August 13, 1937 the Japanese began a three-month battle for the city, suffering nearly 200,000 casualties. It is believed that the tremendous losses suffered by the Japanese during this battle, led to the infamous incident weeks later in Nanking merely 170 miles west of Shanghai.

Variations on the supply and cavalry *sake* cups. $15-$20

Further examples of supply and cavalry *sake* cups. $15-$20

Additional examples of supply and cavalry *sake* cups. $15-$20

Above: Railway *sake* cups. The Japanese fought hard to gain control of the lucrative Russian-built railway through Manchuria. Japanese troops were placed on trains and at key stations to protect this precious asset. Cups with rail engines are rare. $40

9th Regiment supply, victorious return. $20

Rare "Victorious return" cup with rifle and signed flag that states, "Victory in battle, long life." $35

38th Infantry regiment discharge commemorative. The scroll contains the first few lines of the five precepts on a soldier's attributes, as listed in the soldiers duty book (*guntai techo*).

Discharge commemorative, 36th Infantry regiment. Poem reads, "Hold high the glorious regimental colors." $35

3rd anti-aircraft illumination commemorative. $30

Right: 68th machine gun discharge commemorative. Note the soldier aiming at the viewer behind a Type 92, 6.5mm heavy machine gun. $50

Various machine gun *sake* cups. $35-$50

33rd regiment machine gun unit commemorative. $35

Outside of the cup shown above. The outside is embossed with the characters for Discharge commemorative. $35

19th Regiment Shanghai commemorative. Poem reads, "Life is weightless as a feather, Duty is weightier than a mountain." $35

Various cups from the 33rd Infantry Regiment ("*Tsu*" regiment, *see* bottom p. 43) including a flag commemorating the annual regimental color celebration *(gunkisai)*. The 33rd received its regimental standard from the Emperor Meiji on March 24, 1898. In the 1904-1905 Russo-Japanese war, the regiment saw heavy action at the battle for Mukden, Korea. In the China Incident war the regiment was present at the infamous Nanking incident. In the Pacific war the regiment was part of the 16th "Kyoto Division" and participated in the battle for Bataan. It remained on Luzon until April 1944. Under regimental commander Colonel Suzuki's leadership the 33rd regiment was transferred to Leyte in December 1944 where it was outnumbered nearly eighteen-to-one by American troops and destroyed at Tacloban.

Above: Various Manchuria commemorative cups are sought after for their combination of Japanese and the no-longer existing nation of *Manchukuo* flags. $30

6th Infantry, draft commemorative. $25

36th Infantry regiment, discharge commemorative. Poem reads, "Who has not heard of the regiment's actions at the fall of Port Arthur Victory?" $30

18th Infantry Regiment's victorious return from Northern Manchuria. Poem reads, "Life is lighter than a feather, duty is weightier than a mountain." $25

Above: Cover of July 1941 issue of Japanese magazine showing Japanese infantry colors covered in royal purple as it moves through China. (*Shashin Shuho*). $30

1st Imperial Guard electronic communication commemorative. Note the pigeon carrying a message. $30

Nagoya Chindai. During World War II the castle grounds at Nagoya (built by Shogun Tokugawa in 1612) were transformed into an army training facility.

Various Korean commemorative cups. The Japanese gained control over Korea in 1910 and encouraged Japanese immigration to the peninsula. Prior to the Pacific war, an entire generation of Korean born Japanese was raised to serve the Emperor in the military.

Various home leave commemorative *sake* cups. At the outbreak of the Pacific war few Japanese soldiers or sailors received home leave. $25

Various medical *sake* cups. $30

Various rare *sake* cups displaying human figure. $35-$50

Three *sake* cups with figures of soldiers. The cup at the far right has a poem that reads, "With my bayonet I bring peace to the world." $35-$50

Top: Three rare *sake* cups showing soldiers. From left to right: 26th Field artillery, 9th combat engineers China incident, 53rd Infantry maneuvers commemorative. $35-$50 Center: Three *sake* cups with depictions of combat engineers. Of special interest is the cup on the left, whcih shows the infamous three flesh bullet warriors (*nikudan sanyushi*), who gave their lives in a suicidal *bangalore* torpedo attack against defenses at Shanghai on February 22, 1932.

These school children in 1944 are busy polishing the statue commemorating the memory of the "three human bullets" (Pvt's Enoshita, Kitada, and Sakue) who threw themselves and their explosive charge onto a barbed wire defensive position, earning themselves a place in Japanese history. (Shashin shuho). $30

In commemoration of the erecting of the statue of Sgt. Major Himeno. $30

Five gold-washed *kutani* cups. $35

Outside of *kutani* cup Northern China incident commemorative. Note the painstakingly handpainted blue dots. $40

Various aircraft *sake* cups. Note the cup on the bottom left with the early biplane, very rare. $40-$60

Various aircraft *sake* cups. Note the pilot badges. $50

7th flight squadron, commemorative. The 1st Division's 7th army flight squadron was founded in February 1926 at Tokyo's Tachikawa airfield, and moved to the city of Hamamatsu in 1928. In 1933, a training facility was erected to train aircraft maintenance crews and airborne communication crews. The plane depicted on nearly all of the 7th squadron cups encountered is Dornier-designed Type 87 Kawasaki bomber of which only twenty-eight were produced! This bomber was used by the 7th squadron in China in 1931. Members of the 7th squadron also trained in China with dropping gas and chemical weapons from this aircraft. $50

Off to Taiwan commemorative. Cups named to battles are highly desired. $30

Ambassador's resident abroad commemorative, 21st Field artillery. VERY rare. This unit must have been assigned to guard the Japanese ambassador's residence in Manchuria. $50

Right: Occupation of Tientsin, discharge commemorative. $30

Various Imperial Guard *sake* cups. Note the cup at bottom center with crane and turtle motif. The traditional saying is reflected on military cups in hopes for a safe return, "A crane lives 1,000 years, a turtle lives 10,000 years."

33rd Regiment. Bottom of cup has written, "Regiment colors celebration commemorative." $45

3rd Cavalry Regiment. Bottom of cup has written, "Regimental colors celebration commemorative." $35

Three cups for regimental color celebration commemoratives. $35

Outside of the left hand cup in above photo. Regimental color celebration commemorative, December 19, 1929. $35

18th Infantry Regiment commemorative. Note the tattered regimental flag stacked up next to three rifles. The 18th Regiment was wiped out on Saipan. $25

Various China and Manchuria cups. Note the Chinese flag on the upper right cup. $25-$35

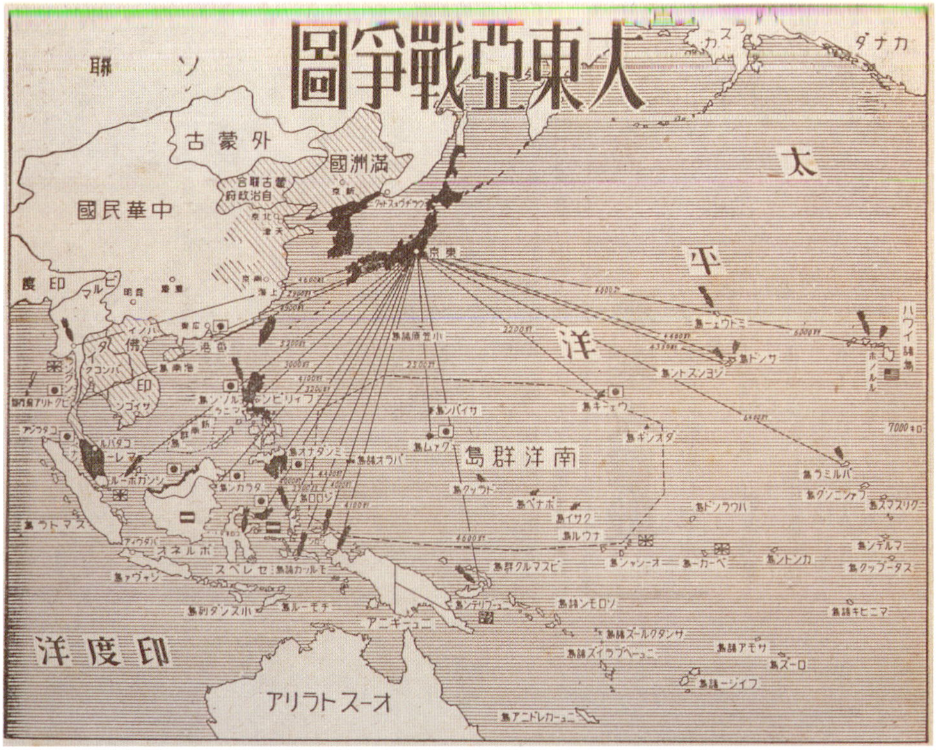

Above: Japanese victories as appearing in Japanese magazine dated February, 1942. (*Shashin Shuho*) Right: Soldier drinking *sake* at discharge ceremony. Note the retired veteran badge and national flag around his chest. (*Shashin Shuho*) $30

Caption reads, "This reclining Buddha matches the attitude of our effortless victories across Asia." From a Japanese propaganda magazine dated March, 1942. (*Shashin Shuho*). $30

Holy War. $25

Right: Greater East Asia Co-prosperity Sphere War. Note the advancing tank on this rare Pacific war cup. $45

Various Pacific war *sake* cups. $40-$50

Pair of Pacific war cups, "Greater East Asia Co-prosperity Sphere War." Note that one of the insets was inserted upside down! A very rare flaw. $75 for the pair

Collection of helmet *sake* cups referred to "*Kabuto sakazuki.*"

Helmet *sake* cups. Left to right top to bottom: a.) 3 artillery shells with characters for "Valor and bravery"; b.) Crossed national and battle flags; c.) 5 shells; d.) cherry blossom atop combat cap style cup; e.) Peaked cap style of cup; f.) National flag. $50

Helmet *sake* cups. Left to right top to bottom: a.) pale green aircraft; b.) Peaked cap style *sake* cup; c.) Unusual pale blue cup; d.) Pale brown light glaze; e.) Character for "Patriotism"; f.) Crossed artillery shells. $50

Helmet *sake* cups. Left to right top to bottom: a.) Naval anchor; b.) Rayed flag; c.) Pale blue combat cap style cup; d.) Three shells with characters for valor and bravery; e.) Unusual swirled pattern; f.) Character for the word "ZAI" of a two cup set that when placed together read "BANZAI." $50

Helmet *sake* cups. Left to right top to bottom: a.) Rayed flag; b.) Three shells "Bravery, Valor"; c.) 5 cherry blossom petals "Patriotism"; d.) "Loyalty"; e.) Peaked cap style of cup; f.) National flag. $50

Right: Helmet cups. Left to right, top to bottom: a.) Five shells; b.) "Glory of the Nation"; c.) "Patriotism" and poem reading, "Return to the homeland and view the wild mountain cherry blossoms."; d.) Military pack design on outside of cup, very unusual. $50

Helmet *sake* cup. Left to right, top to bottom: a.) Double cherry blossoms; b.) Raised soldiers pulling artillery across China; c.) Shape of summer tanker helmet; d.) Raised leaves; e.) Raised star on cherry blossom; f.) "Loyalty" raised blossoms and helmet. $50

Helmet cups. Left to right, top to bottom: a.) "Patriotism" and poem reading, "Return to the homeland and view the wild mountain cherry blossoms."; b.) Airplane; c.) Naval officer; d.) "Glory of the Nation" with raised map of China; e.) "Glory of the Nation" with raised map of China; f.) "Invincible." $50

Helmet cups. Left to right, top to bottom: a.) five blossoms; b.) Airplane "Imperial Forces"; c.) Two cherry blossoms; d.) Crossed rifles over railway tie; e.) Raised retired military badge, cup is made of ultra rare Bakelite; f.) Crossed shells. $50

Close-up of helmet cup in combat cap style. Note chinstrap and vent holes. $50

Close-up of military pack style helmet cup. $50

Left: Close-up of cup with raised tank, ship and Type 11 machine gun. Note the patent pending marking. $40

Grouping of army and naval *sake* bottles. *Sake* bottles have also been found made from metal, and with caps that serve as cups, as well as pointed caps that cause the bottles to resemble bullets.

Grouping of six army bottles. $50

Grouping of six army bottles. $50

Grouping of six naval bottles. $50

Grouping of six army bottles. A *sake* bottle would normally hold .18 liters of alcohol and were referred to by their capacity of "1 Go." $50

Sake tray, "1st Imperial guard communications." Note the radio flag and the map symbol for communications at the top left of the tray. $60

Sake tray, "68th Infantry, Glory of the Nation." Named to "Toyama." $50

Sake tray with helmet and combat cap, "China Incident commemorative." Poem reads, "You have dedicated your life in service of the Emperor, return now to the homeland to view the flowers." $75

Sake tray, "Naval term fulfillment commemorative." Note the gold wash forming waves around the battleship. $100

Sake tray, "Naval term fulfillment commemorative." Note the artillery shell, anchor, and cherry blossom branch. $100

Boxed *sake* tray, "4th Imperial guard discharge commemorative." $100

Sake warmer, "Banzai to the Empire." $50

Sake bottle resting on *sake* warmer. The warmer would house a small candle lit to keep the beverage warm. $100

Left: Boxed "Medical Unit discharge commemorative." $45

Four boxed lacquer cups. $65-$95

Left: Boxed lacquer cup with map of Japan sea. $75

Four boxed reserve veteran *sake* cups. $65-$85

Set of five cups with soldier's attributes, read right to left top to bottom: 1. *Gunjin wa chuusetsu* (A soldier is Loyal); 2. *Gunjin wa reigi* (A soldier is Polite); 3. *Gunjin wa Buyu* (A soldier is Brave); 4. *Gunjin wa Shingi* (A soldier is Trustworthy); 5. *Gunjin wa Shiso* (A soldier is Thrifty). $100

Two boxed lacquer cups. $65

Very rare paper box for *sake* cup, "Commemorative *sake* cup." $25

Set of three cups with raised tray (translation). $125

Three anti-aircraft *sake* cups and their counterparts still wrapped in period newspaper. $35

Rare hinged boxed set of matched bottles and cups. $150

Six lacquered cups. $35-$50

A pair of rare lacquer *sake* cups Golden Kite medal and brown exterior with 1905 era officer's sword. $50

Right: "Given by the Emperor for Large Scale Exercises." Cups presented by the Emperor are highly sought after and known as "Shihai." $40

Eight lacquer *sake* cups left to right, top to bottom: a.) Discharge commemorative, Headquarters 33rd Infantry Regiment; b.) "*Shinpu*" (Swing the Sword) for *Kamikaze* pilots; c.) "13th Battalion Discharge, Matsumoto"; d.) Presented to "1st Private *Nagashima*; e. f. g. h.) Set of cups presented by the Emperor for "Personal bodyguard of the Emperor large scale maneuvers, 1925." $40

Left: Lacquer cup with drawing of *Kawanishi* flying boat. Outside says, "Commemorative of *Kawanishi* Manufacturing." $50

Six cups, five of which are for large-scale military maneuvers. Bottom far right shows a military reserve commemorative. $40

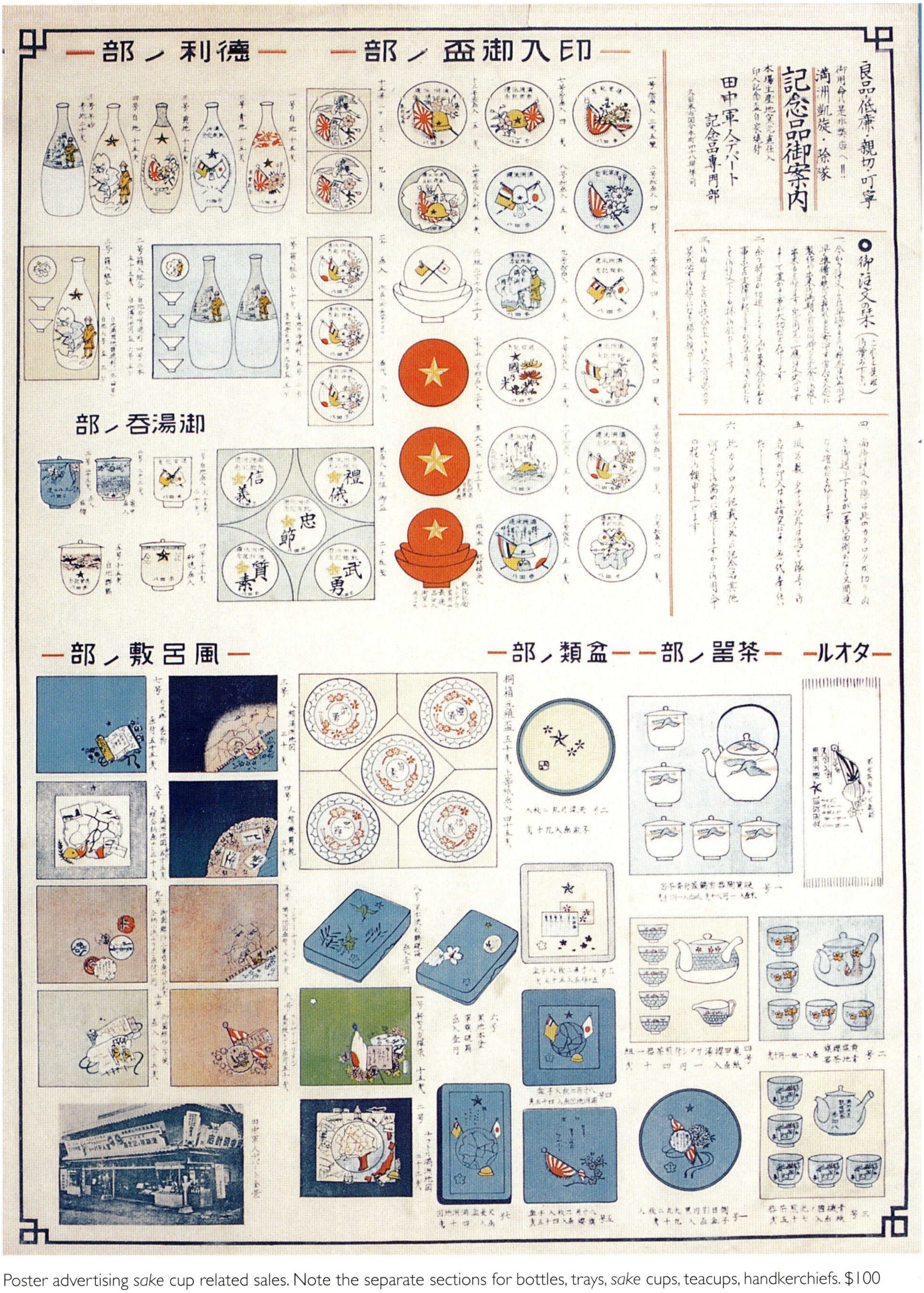

Poster advertising *sake* cup related sales. Note the separate sections for bottles, trays, *sake* cups, teacups, handkerchiefs. $100

Tin *sake* cup with gold wash, Order of the Golden Kite breast badge. $40

Very rare metal *sake* cup with Admiral *Kamiura*. Note the English! $50

Metal cup, Valor and war deeds, Russo-Japan war. $40

Metal Japanese (*ocha*) teacup coaster, "Discharge commemorative." Note the regimental front gate. $30

Japanese tea (*ocha*) cup with marks-manship award. $40

Child's rice bowl with flag and tank. $25

1905 era patriotic 1st battalion civilian rice bowl. $25

Pair of commemorative tea cups, "Discharge commemorative." $30

Sake cup with soldier standing on Great Wall of China. $35

Set of candy coasters for use with Japanese thick bitter green tea. "Valor war deeds" The back of the coasters is embossed, "1st Lieutenant *Yamanishi*." $40

Naval shipboard officer's coffee cup. $75

Merchant Marine shipboard English tea cup, brought home from war by Lt. Commander Percy Dunkle, USN. The bottom of the cup says in English "Meito China" and in Japanese kanji says "Ceramic made in Nagoya" A very unusual piece! $50

Left: Naval shipboard western soup bowl from officer's mess. $45

Naval shipboard *Miso* soup bowls from officers' messes. $45

Toothpick holder from Japanese pub with original toothpicks. $35

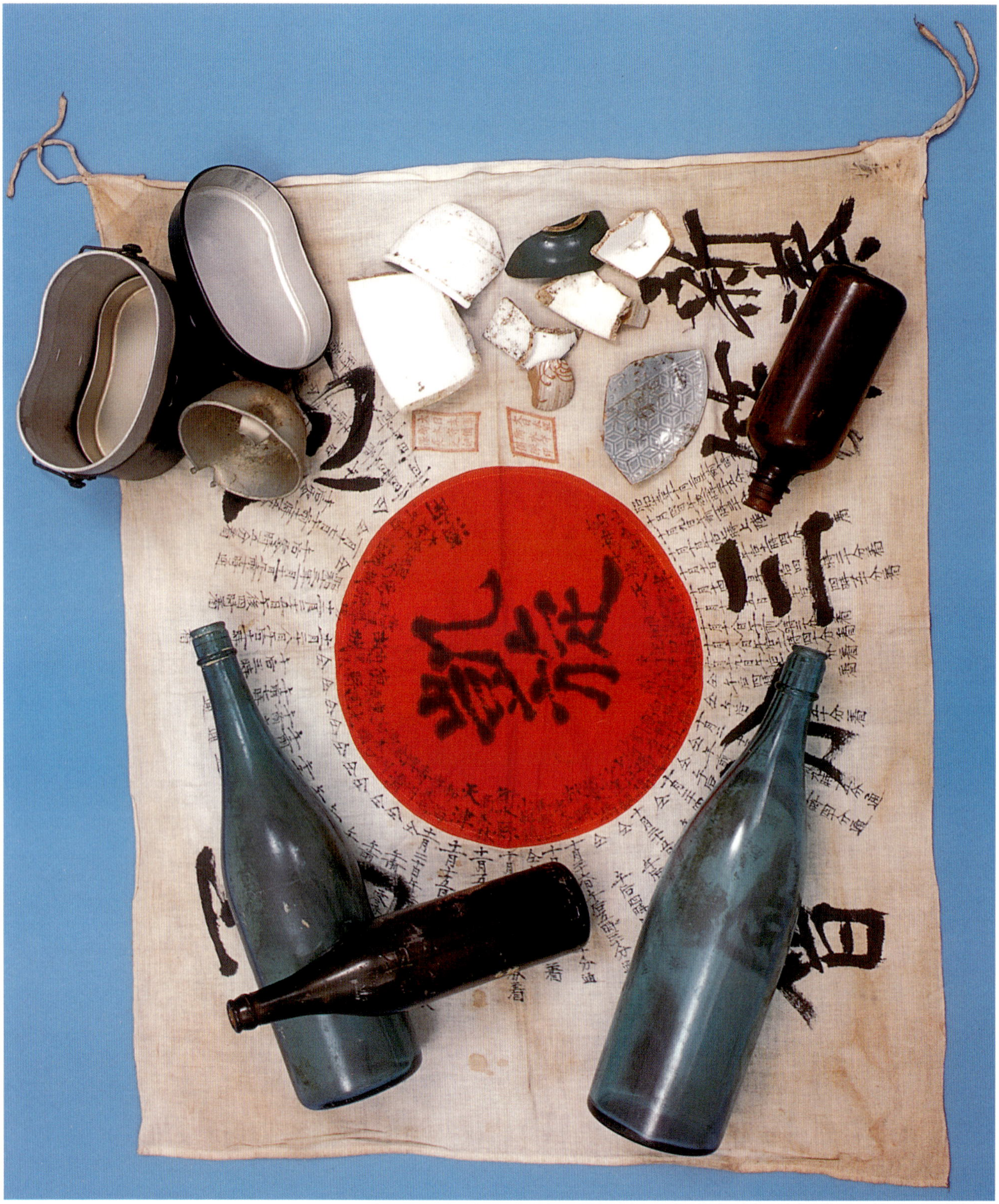

Grouping of *sake* bottles, trays, dishes and cups author has found across Pacific battlesites. As is evident in photos, soldiers in the field would drink *sake* from mess tin lids, metal and ceramic bowls, and drinking glasses. The large green *sake* bottles hold 1.8 liters of *sake* and are referred to by their capacity, "1 Shou."

"Army officer academy at Toyama."
$35

"Army infantry school detachment commemorative." $30

"Army infantry school detachment commemorative, Miyata." $30

Sake cup with Emperor on horseback. $25

Emperor *Hirohito* on his steed "Snow white." (*Shashin Shuho*)

"Discharge commemorative, Tokyo *KEMPEITAI, Kubota*." $100

Very rare KIA *sake* cup: "In memory of the late Army Infantry *Private Yasujji Wada*, death in battle commemorative." $150

天佑ヲ保有シ萬世一系ノ帝祚ヲ践メル
大日本帝國天皇ハ内　藤　績ヲ
明治勲章ノ勲八等ニ叙シ白色桐葉
章ヲ授與ス即チ此位ニ屬スル禮遇及ヒ
特權ヲ有セシム
神武天皇即位紀元二千六百年
昭和十五年四月二十九日宮城ニ於テ
璽ヲ鈐セシム

昭和十五年四月二十九日

賞勲局總裁従三位勲一等　下條康麿

第三百七十九万二千八百十七號ヲ以テ
勲等簿冊ニ記入ス

賞勲局書記官正六位勲五等　村田八千穂

Rising Sun 8th Class medal award document dated April 29, 1940. $65

Sake cup commemorating award of the Rising Sun 7th class, named to Tanaka. $35

Pair of *sake* cups with rare price tag still attached! The cost of the cup is listed at "6 sen," which was equal to the cost of a bottle of *sake*. $40

"19th regiment home leave commemorative." $25

Sets of three *sake* cups. Note the bugle. $75

Sets of three *sake* cups. $75

"Six week temporary recall commemorative." $25

"One year temporary recall commemorative." $20

"9th regiment." Note the unusual spike placed in the center of the cup – its use is unknown. $20

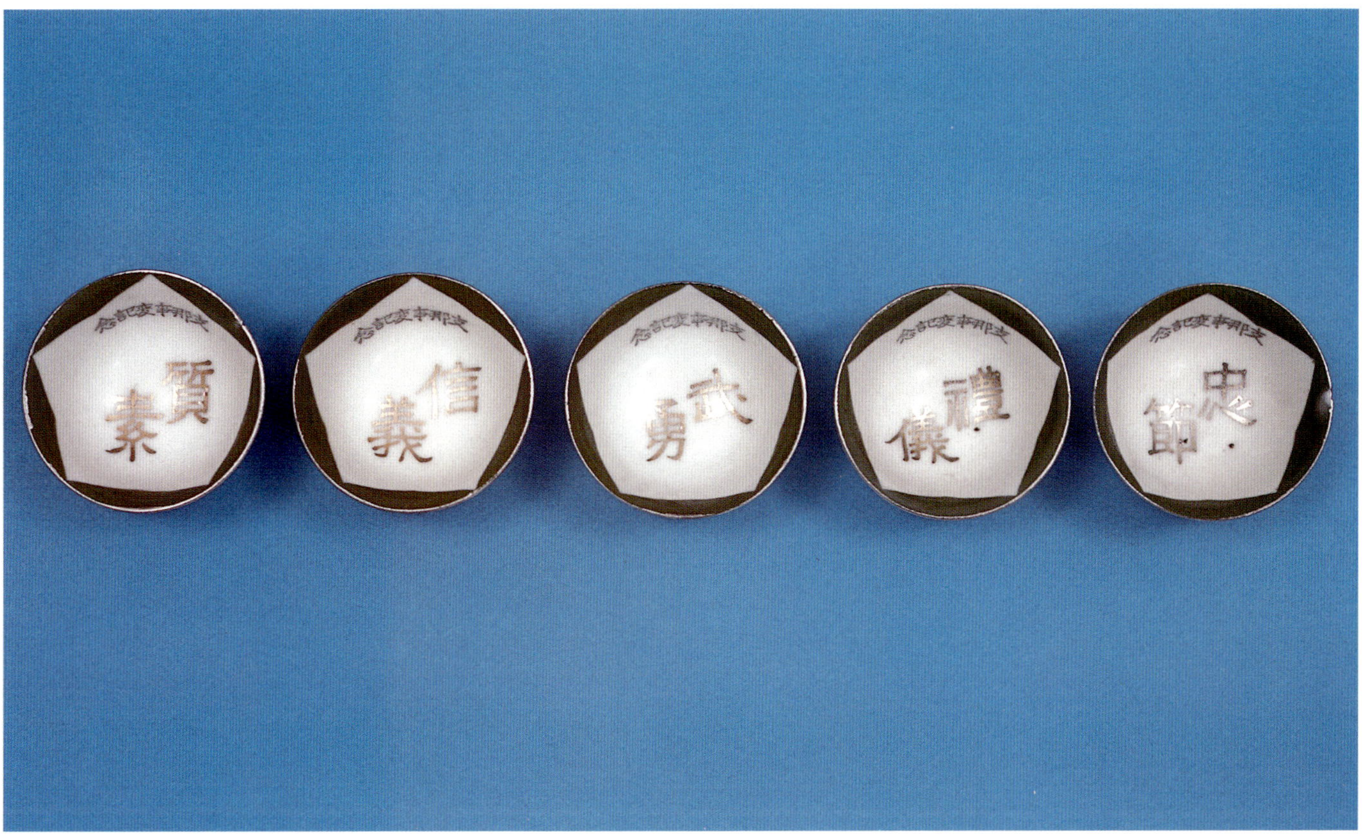

Set of five *sake* cups with the attributes for the Imperial soldier: 1. *Gunjin wa chuusetsu* (A soldier is Loyal); 2. *Gunjin wa reigi* (A soldier is Polite); 3. *Gunjin wa Buyu* (A soldier is Brave); 4. *Gunjin wa Shingi* (A soldier is Trustworthy); 5. *Gunjin wa Shiso* (A soldier is Thrifty). $100

Type 96 artillery gun in action in China. (*Shashin Shuho*)

Various artillery and field artillery *sake* cups. $25-$35

"20th field artillery discharge." Note the retired veterans badge. $30

Various artillery and field artillery *sake* cups. $25-$35

Various artillery and field artillery *sake* cups. $25-$35

Various artillery and field artillery *sake* cups. $25-$35

Above: Six naval cups. Of interest is the cup on top far right from the Cruiser *NAMA*(?). Tour to America commemorative. Prior to World War II, Japan's navy made goodwill trips to foreign countries handing out sample foods, cap tallies, and souvenirs. $45

"Warship Fuso home leave commemorative." The name for the warship *Fuso* was taken from ancient Chinese literature's description of Japan as being the land of the rising of the sun. The *Fuso* was lost at the battle of Leyte Gulf in 1945. $45

Six "naval term fulfillment" cups. $40

Various naval term fulfillment cups. $40

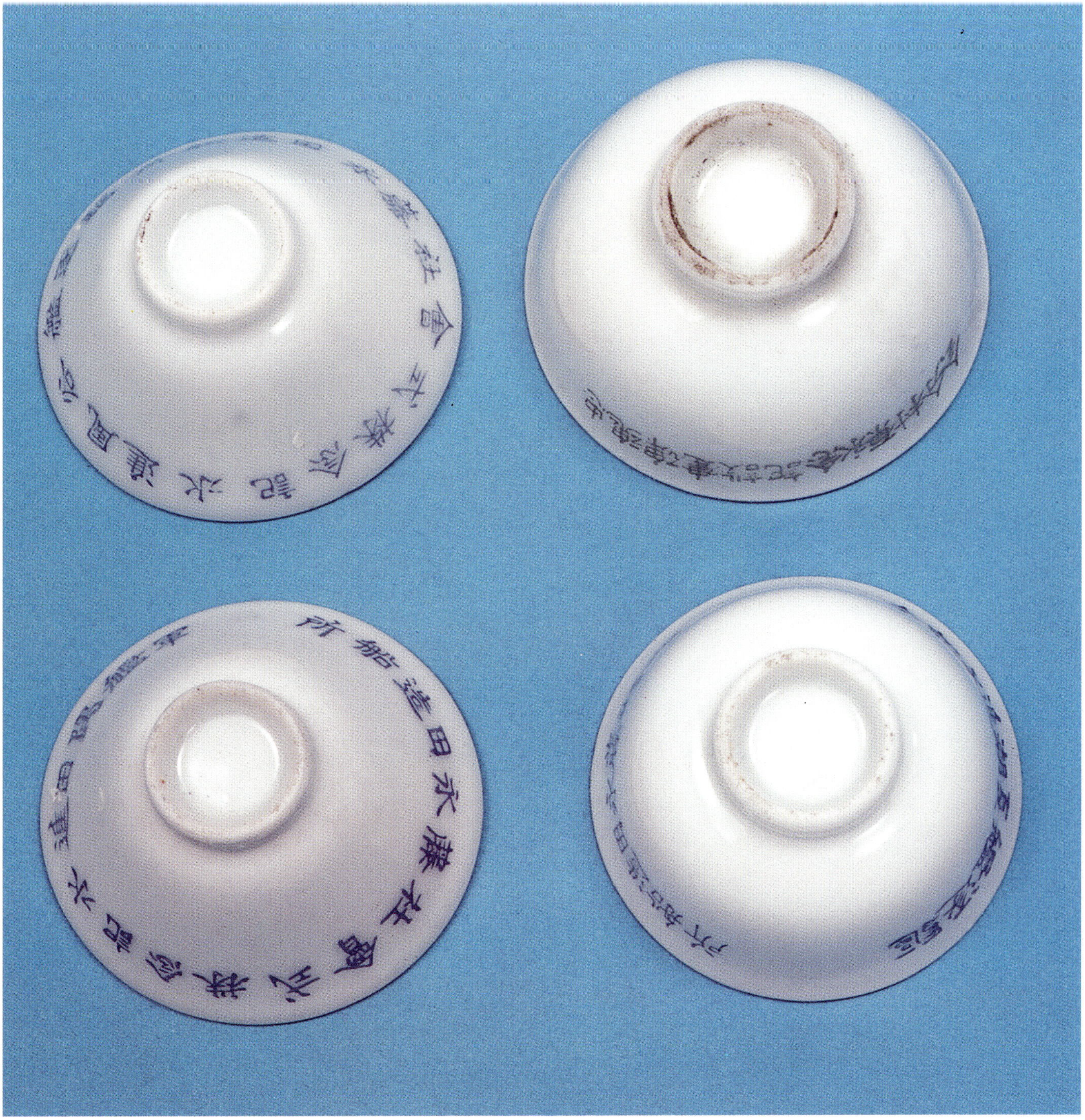

Naval ship launching commemorative cups

a) "Commemorative of ship launching Destroyer *Tanikaze* by the Fujinagata ship building Corp"The *Kagero* class *Tanikaze* was completed in April 1941. The *Tanikaze* distinguished itself by participating in the Pearl Harbor attack, the fall of Wake Island, Rabaul, bombardment of Christmas Island south of Hawaii, Midway, Solomon, Santa Cruz, evacuation of Guadalcanal until it was torpedoed and sunk in the Philippines on June 9, 1944 by the U.S. submarine SS-257. $50

b) "Commemorative of ship launching for Destroyer *Natsushio* by the Fujinagata ship building Corp" The *Kagero* class *Natsuhio* was built in August 1940 and sunk on February 9, 1942 (during the Japanese landing at the battle of Makassar Indonesia). The *Natsushio* was torpedoed and sunk by the U.S. submarine SS-37 (Lt. Dempsey) in Makassar Strait causing the only Japanese naval loss in the entire action. $50

c) "Commemorative of ship launching for the gunboat Sumida by the Fujinagata ship building Corp." The gunboat *Sumida* was completed in 1906 by Thornycraft in England. It was refitted in Japan in 1942 just prior to the Battle of Midway. $45

d) "Nagahara village war dead shrine commemorative." $40

Above: Various "Naval term fulfillment" *sake* cups. $40

"Naval engineering 1st Lieutenant." Shown three times normal size. $50

Above: Various "naval term fulfillment" *sake* cups. Note the pagoda style superstructures, indicative of Japanese warships. $40

"Naval victorious return commemoratives." $40

"Naval term fulfillment commemoratives." Note the aircraft. $40

"Naval term fulfillment commemoratives." Note the metal *sake* cup for the very rare annual engineering proficiency award badge. $100

"Naval term fulfillment commemoratives." $40

"Naval term fulfillment commemoratives." $40

"Naval term fulfillment commemoratives." $40

"Naval term fulfillment commemoratives." Of interest is the upper left cup for the "1st combined fleet", and the other cup on the bottom right with a samurai family crest. $35

Above: "Naval term fulfillment commemoratives." $40

Close-up of "Overseas cruise to USA and England commemorative." $40

Above: American "flappers" taste Japanese food aboard ship in New York harbor, circa 1935. Note the Japanese officer and enlisted ranks looking over their shoulders grinning. (*Shashin Shuho*)

"Naval term fulfillment commemorative." Note the aircraft. $40

"Naval term fulfillment commemoratives." Note the gunnery insignia of torpedo and cannon. $40

Battleship surrounded by goodluck cranes. $35

"Naval term fulfillment commemoratives." $40

Japanese pagoda style battleship. (*Shashin Shuho*) $15

"Naval term fulfillment commemoratives." Note the broken cup commemorating the world cruise of the transport/seaplane tender *Soya*. When the *Soya* took her "around the world cruise" in 1910 she had 1st Lt. Isoroku Yamamoto aboard. Even though this cup is broken, it is of significant historical value. In May 1942, the *Soya* left Saipan and Wake bound to re-supply the expected Japanese invasion of Midway, but was turned back. It did, however, participate in the battle of Guadalcanal in November 1942. $35

"Naval combat engineers." $40

Traditional *sake* barrels, and the Yasukuni war shrine.

BIBLIOGRAPHY

Nihon Rikugun Butai Souran (Shinjin butsu juraisha, 1998)

Nihon Rikugun Rentai Souran (Shinjin butsu juraisha, 1990)

Taiheiyou Sensou Rentai Senshi ((Shinjin butsu juraisha, 2000)

Ground Power, Organization of Japanse Armored Units, (Delta Shupan, 2001)

America Betrayed, by Guy Gabaldon
(Self published—The 1950s WWII movie "Hell to Eternity" was based on his life story.)

Nihon Gunso Shashin Shu Vol. 1 (Nihon Gunso Kenkyukai, 2000)

Taiheiyou Senseki Irei Souran ((Shinjin butsu juraisha, 1998)

Peterson,James. *Orders and Medals of Japan and Associated States*. O.M.S.A. Monograph 1, 1994.